UNDERSTANDING THE
POWER OF
FASTING
WITH
PRAYER

ANENA MARIA GORETTI

MINISTRY IN ART PUBLISHING
communicating excellence

PRESENTED TO

_____

OCCASION

_____

PRESENTED BY

_____

DATE

_____

Ministry In Art Publishing Ltd
e-mail: publishing@ministryinart.com
www.miapublishing.com

ISBN: 978-1-907402-05-0

Cover design:
www.miadesign.com

DEDICATION

This book is dedicated to God the Father, the Son and the Holy Spirit; thank you for drawing me closer and closer to you, over the years my love for you has grown deeper and deeper. As the deer pants for the water brooks, so pants my soul for You, O God.

Daddy, I am forever grateful to you for saving my life and calling me to be your daughter and servant, to you I ascribe greatness! You are the lifter of my head, my helper, my deliverer, the one and only God I worship. Thank you for depositing wisdom in me. Through the many trials you have brought me through, you taught me how to pray and fast, and I thank you for releasing me to share this knowledge with your people. How you entrusted me with this knowledge amazes me! Indeed you are full of grace, what an honor to walk in your grace!

You have brought me through some battles that caused me to enter into seasons of prayer and spiritual warfare that propelled me to break through the glass ceiling in my prayer life.

Who shall separate me from your love? Shall tribulation, or distress, or persecution, or famine, or nakedness, or peril, or sword? No! Nothing Lord. I have encountered so much but I have seen your grace see me through. To you alone I give glory and honor, you are beautiful beyond description.

"Now to the King eternal, immortal, invisible, to God who alone is wise, be honor and glory forever and ever. Amen."

With Lots of Love,

Anena Maria Goretti

ACKNOWLEGDMENT

I am deeply grateful to my spiritual father Dr. Albert Odulele who laboured tirelessly over me to bring me where I am today. God sent you into my life when I was in a valley of confusion and fear, but your words of wisdom and prayers upheld me and brought me out. Thank you for your love, you will forever shine.

To Mrs. Bose Odulele, you are a mother to Israel, thank you for all the calls you make to encourage me, I count it a privilege.

Dr. Josephine Kyambadde, my mentor, where do I start from? You are such an inspiration, I am grateful for your love. Thank you so much; you are one in a million, thank you for holding my hand and guiding me through the course of fulfilling my mandate on earth. Thank you for the many hours you spent with me putting this book together, for the great ideas and wisdom, and for throwing the rock that helped me break through. You were a necessary component in the birthing of this book, you will forever increase and your head will not lack oil.

Pastor Peter Kyambadde, you are a true friend and mentor, thank you for your counsel and words of encouragement. Thank you for believing in me. You have been such a tremendous support, and I appreciate you very much.

Pastors Matthew and Yemisi Ashimolowo, I look up to you. Your lives are an inspiration to me, and your teachings have moulded, revived, and challenged me. May my God bless you and continue to uphold you. Generations and generations to come will celebrate you.

Indeed it was not a mistake that I met you Bishop Annie Njeri, but true divine intervention. You have added to my life; thank you for mentoring me. You are a gem.

Pastors Clem and Marjorie Esomowei, God's battle axes; it is an honour to be mentored by you both. You will grow from strength to strength, amen.

Apostle Israel and Pastor Beatrice Owusu-Ansah, I still remember the prophetic words you spoke over me to put me on the course of fulfilling my Destiny. Thank you for your love, support and wise counsel. I salute you both.

Apostle Julius Oyet, thank you for your prayers and support, I appreciate you. God bless you and all yours richly.

Pastors Richard and Lilian Odoch, thank you for your love and prayers, God bless you abundantly.

Rev. Francis and Margaret Bompoh, God bless you for your prayers and the continuous support you have given to my life and ministry.

Pastors Daniel and Angela Ayettey, thank you for always being there, you both are such a tremendous support, God greatly bless you and all yours.

Pastor Benedicta Olagunju, you are a unique woman and a treasure to our generation congratulations!

Thank you for your prayers and words of encouragement, God bless you woman of God.

Rev. Funke Adetuberu, you are an epistle that I always read, my life has been transformed into Christ's nature because of your teachings, God bless you forever.

Pastor Sarah Morgan, the prophetic word you gave me has pushed me this far, may God's favour always go before and after you.

My love goes to my one and only precious daughter, Fiona Goretti, thank you for encouraging me and supporting me in different ways. Mighty woman of God; may my God bless you and remember all your good works.

My grandson Omari Caleb Jamal, I can never forget when you came and asked, "Grandma, can I please help you type, I am very good at it." I was shocked to hear you say that, at just five years old you were willing to be supportive. You will go places in Jesus' name. Great man of God, nations are waiting for you, well done.

My adopted son, Simon Blessing, GCD Orphans Uganda and Kenya, Widows with Strength Uganda and Kenya, thank you for your prayer support, you will not lack any good thing.

Reverend Abraham and Hannah Usikaro thank you for your prayers and encouragement.

Dr. Femi Olowo, the Principal of South London Bible College, my immense gratitude for the training in Ministry; may God continue to enlarge your coast.

Pastors Luis and Marie Jeanne Arku

Ran and Julia Young, thank you for your support and prayers, God bless you.

Pastor Susan Noreen, Dr. Curdel Mcload, Dr. Ofori, Pastor Esther Carnegie, you have all been my wonderful encouragers. Indeed on that day Christ will whisper these special words in your ears, "Well done good and faithful servants"

Thank you Dr. Mmieh and Mrs. Constance for believing in me and accepting me as one of your own, God bless you.

Uncle Orlando and Sister Doris and the entire family. Thank you for all your love and support of my family. God bless you.

Pastor Grace Shola Oludoyi, your smile is so anointed it always encourages me, along with all your beautiful words of encouragement; thank you my sister.

Pastor Yemi Adeleke, you are an inspiration; your presence at the Total Woman Conferences has sharpened me and made me a good and godly woman. I love and respect you.

Sincere thanks to sister Damaris Kamau, you have helped me in many ways; you stayed awake for hours to give me company as I wrote this book, may you live to see many more glorious years to come.

I tried typing this manuscript but I couldn't, many thanks to Karen Johnson and Vivian Johnson for availing yourselves for the Master's use. Your gift of typing has been a blessing.

June Coldwell, thank you for all your words of encouragement all through the process of putting this book together, I am eternally grateful.

Minister Vivienne Wilson, Sonia Thompson, Gloria Tabi, Sarah Kuwornu. Eternity will celebrate you. Thanks to all members of Acts Ministries International for supporting me with your prayers and love that have kept me going. You are such a wonderful congregation.

Thank you Revelation and Esther Ayigbe for your counsel and prayers, from the time I gave my heart to the Lord you have been a source of strength in my walk with the Lord.

Abi, my editor, you will live and reign with Christ. Many thanks for the great work you have done, your advice and wisdom are paramount.

Sister Petua Akom, thank you for sowing seeds of God's Word in my life, you will forever be above your enemies.

Grace Birikorang, I can never forget how you travailed for my salvation, thank you for also inviting me to my first conference where I received deliverance.

The prayers you offered for my salvation reached the throne room of God, thank you Rev. Chigbundu, I can never imagine where I would be today without Christ.

Bishop Donnet and Rev. Alison and the entire congregation of Power of the Living Word International, London, thank you for your prayers and support.

I also want to appreciate all of you who believe in me and my God-given call; God bless you, I love you all.

To all my family members, especially my aunt Epifania Akwongo who introduced me to God, you always said this to me, and it has remained with me, "Goretti you are an orphan, know that God is your Father; wherever you may be in the world, when you are in trouble call on Him!!! I will not always be with you." I am forever grateful. May the Lord Jesus reward you abundantly above all that you ask or think. You have given me a firm and a sure foundation which is Christ the solid rock on which I stand.

CONTENTS

Acknowlegdment 7

Foreword...19

Introduction 23

CHAPTER I
   CALL TO TRUE FASTING 29

CHAPTER II
   PRAYER 37

CHAPTER III
   CONSISTENT PRAYER 43

CHAPTER IV
   CHALLENGE..51

CHAPTER V
   HEARING GOD DURING
   FASTING 55

CHAPTER VI
   THE KEY TO OPEN HEAVEN..............................65

CHAPTER VII
   DURATION OF FASTING 71

CHAPTER VIII
   GUIDELINES TO FASTING...................................85

CHAPTER IX
BENEFIT OF FASTING 91

CHAPTER X
"WAITING" - ISAIAH 40: 28-31 101

CHAPTER XI
LEARNING FROM THE EAGLE........................ 113

CHAPTER XII
MORE LESSONS ON THE EAGLE 125

CHAPTER XIII
MISCONCEPTIONS ABOUT FASTING........... 135

CHAPTER XIV
PROPHETIC DECLARATION 141

FOREWORD

In my view, great moral, medical, military and monetary maladies beset our world and it's time believers seek the face of the Lord as never before. Christians must awake to their God given covenants and enforce the will of God in their communities and personal lives. The challenges of the 21st century are unmistakeable, and spiritual weapons of warfare are required to counter them. Clearly, the devil is on a rampage of death, dearth and destruction and the souls of men are being held captive.

The bible aptly describes our times in 2 Timothy 3:1-7:

But know this, that in the last days perilous times will come: For men will be lovers of themselves, lovers of money, boasters, proud, blasphemers, disobedient to parents, unthankful, unholy, unloving, unforgiving, slanderers, without self-control, brutal, despisers of good, traitors, headstrong, haughty, lovers of pleasure rather than lovers of

God, having a form of godliness but denying its power. And from such people turn away! For of this sort are those who creep into households and make captives of gullible women loaded down with sins, led away by various lusts'

There are realms of spiritual power and authority inaccessible to those unwilling to exercise themselves regularly in fasting and prayer. Jesus fasted and prayed for forty days and nights and afterwards 'returned in the power of the Spirit to Galilee, and news of Him went out through the entire surrounding region' Luke 4:14. To destroy the bands of wickedness, dispel generational holds over nations and establish the kingdom of God in all spheres requires prayers and fasting. Jesus said, 'this kind can come out by nothing but prayer and fasting' Mark 9:29.

'Understanding the Power of Fasting with Prayer' is not just another book on the subject. It is a comprehensive, practical and indispensible resource for anyone who has decided to experience the true power of God. Drawing from sound biblical insight, first hand experience and deep-seated conviction, Anena Maria Goretti makes a passionate call to all believers to return to the ancient Christian practice of fasting and prayer.

Fasting is not a popular subject; particularly in a world of fast foods, entertainment, recreation and pleasure. Nonetheless, the author approaches the subject with the courage of a mandated messenger, the credibility of a regular practitioner and a conviction that stems from a record of several victories. This book is balanced, practical and a wholesome treatise. It is both incisive and easy to read, taking the individual on an instructional yet inspiring journey.

I recommend this book wholeheartedly. Fasting and prayer, fortified by practical understanding, will tackle longstanding frustrations, terminate strong adversity, break foul habits and release the rich blessings of God.

Congratulations, this is the beginning of a great voyage into all that God has in store for you.

Dr Albert Odulele
Glory House Churches International

INTRODUCTION

Fasting is perhaps the hardest and most counter-cultural of all the spiritual disciplines. Sensibly and prayerfully, I encourage you to explore fasting as a means to help you grow to be more like Jesus. Fasting draws us closer to God because it enables us to experience a deeper relationship with Him. Like Anna, in Luke 2:37, whose example we ought to emulate, fasting should be a life style. "...but served God with fastings and prayers night and day."

As you read this God given revelation, you will discover that fasting is divine when done with the right motive. The purpose of a spiritual fast is to focus upon God and worship Him, not to lose weight, go on a hunger strike or save money on food. NO! It goes beyond that. It is about feeding the spirit through our obedience to God. My prayer is that I will inspire you or help you understand the act of fasting and how it can help you grow closer to God as you pray and focus. There are many benefits of prayer and fasting, and as we look at these benefits they will push you in prayer and encourage you to fast. **Fasting can be challenging** but I want to assure you that it has so many benefits that will make you grateful that you obeyed the voice of God. Believe me, I do not want to lie to you by telling you that when God calls me to fast I throw a party or rejoice, no way! It is a sacrifice, God does not demand you to fast, He does not force Himself on you. He has given you a will, it's up to you to obey Him and please your Father and Maker. Fasting is good, profitable, and beneficial.

When I was attacked by the devil, the Holy Sprit led me into prayer with fasting, the results were phenomenal. He told me to slow down and spend quality time with Him. This world is in too much of a hurry, and God's will is best known when you can "be still and know that I am God." How can you be "STILL?" It is simply by setting aside quality time in prayer with fasting.

The purpose of fasting is to take our eyes off the things of this world to focus completely on God. Fasting is a way to demonstrate to God and to ourselves, that we are serious about our relationship with Him. Fasting helps us gain a new perspective and a renewed reliance upon God.

By taking our eyes off the things of this world, we can more successfully turn our attention to God. Fasting is not a way to get God to do what we want. Through fasting, God changes us. Fasting is not a way to appear more spiritual than others, rather it is an act that gets us closer to God when done in a spirit of humility with a joyful attitude.

"Moreover, when you fast, do not be like the hypocrites, with a sad countenance. For they disfigure their faces that they may appear to men to be fasting. Assuredly, I say to you, they have their reward. But you, when you fast, anoint your head and wash your face, so that you do not appear to men to be fasting, but to your Father who is in the secret place; and your Father who sees in secret will reward you openly." Matthew 6:16-18 NKJV.

If there was ever an hour for prayer and fasting, it is now! The church today lacks unction, it is powerless because it is prayerless, our prayer meetings are either dead or dying. The moral decay of the nations continues to rise, and the church appears to be asleep. It seems she has no awareness that she has been called to be a soldier and that this Christian walk with God is warfare. Do you really pray and fast? Are you crying out in prayer for God's visitation? If not, why not? What is your excuse? Come on! You can do all things through Christ who strengthens you. Join me on this walk of prayer with fasting and your life will never remain the same.

Stay blessed,

Anena Maria Goretti

Understanding The Power
Of
Fasting With Prayer

Chapter One

CALL TO TRUE FASTING

The call to true fasting with prayer arises when you have a deep cause and a realistic reason to fast. When you are praying for a situation and you experience a demonic interference and appear not to break through then you add fasting. Jesus said to His disciples in Mark 9:29 "This kind can come forth by nothing; but by prayer and fasting." It could be that you are seeking God for direction in a particular area of your life or ministry. God said in Proverbs 3:6, in all our ways we should acknowledge him, and he shall direct our paths. You don't have to make the same mistake Joshua made when the Gibeonites deceived him; instead of seeking the face of the Lord to find out if what they were saying was true, Joshua just made peace with them and allowed them to live with the Israelites only to find out after three days that they were their neighbours. It was a rather sad situation because Joshua and the Israelites couldn't do anything to them since they had sworn to them in the name of Jehovah God to let them be.

Is this not what we all do? In one way or the other we often end up doing the same thing Joshua did. But when we go to God in prayer with fasting, God is able to direct or warn us. For example, He might say, "That is not the way," or "go ahead this is my will."

I can identify with Joshua. I once encountered a similar situation where someone came to me and said that God had spoken to them to come and help me with the work of the ministry. It was like the golden answer from heaven. You know when you have been praying for a long time and suddenly it looks like everything seems to be falling into place, not knowing it was a lie. I never bothered to seek God about it, by the time I realised it the damage had been done and that was when I remembered to call on God. You know our God is a Father and we are His children; when I did call on Him, He received me with open arms and picked me up from my mistakes; He gave me a second chance by pointing me in the right direction.

After going through that experience I was led to ponder on the verse below;

"For day after day they seek me out; they seem eager to know my ways, as if they were a nation that does what is right and has not forsaken the commands of its God. They ask me for just decisions and seem eager for God to come near them"
Isaiah 58:2

Look at the Israelites in the above scripture; they fasted, they asked for just decisions, they humbled themselves. They seemed eager to know God's ways and to do what was right. However, even though they did these things they were not being heard.

The reason for this is revealed. They were doing these things not to please God, but to please themselves, their hearts were not right. What they were doing had become mere ritual, mere activity, something they were doing for themselves. On the days they fasted, they ended up arguing and fighting. Read Isaiah 58:3-4. Today, some of us have fallen into this. We view our walk with God as a one-day-a-week commitment. Sometimes when we go to church, we expect it to be a time that is just for us.

We become wrapped up in the things of man, not the things of God.

True fasting means having a pure heart, it is important that God works on our hearts because He hates stony hearts; He is looking for a heart that is submissive to His will and His ways so that He can use us. Let us continue to look at this verse below;

"Is this not the fast that I have chosen: To loose the bonds of wickedness, To undo the heavy burdens, To let the oppressed go free…Is it not to share your bread with the hungry, And that you bring to your house the poor who are cast out… Then your light shall break forth like the morning, Your healing shall spring forth speedily… Isaiah 58:6-9

Now we see the fast that God has chosen. It's not a time to honour yourself, but a time to think of others. The fast God has chosen is a time to clothe the naked, to do away with injustices, to feed the hungry, and to provide shelter for the homeless. It is to love your neighbour as yourself. This is what I call true fasting.

When you do those things, your light will go before you. God will honour, bless, and preserve you. When you glorify God with these actions, others will see it. A city on a hill cannot be hidden. The glory of the Lord will be your rear guard. That is an amazing promise. And when you call, He will answer. When you do away with the pointing finger and with serving only yourself, and when you bring relief to the oppressed, the Lord will provide for you. He will strengthen you to do great things. When the Lord's will is a delight to you, you will find your joy in the Him, for "the mouth of the LORD" has spoken it.

This is all about not serving ourselves but serving God. Sometimes it is hard to recognize when we do this, but the truth is we are called to serve God and serve Him with humility, just like Joshua laid the Lord's command before the people that they should fear Him and serve only Him. Jesus spoke about true fasting with prayer in Matthew 6:1-18, it is done not for the purpose of outward show but so that you may be drawn into a deeper relationship with Him that will express harmony with His blessings and His intention to forgive. Fasting is a way to demonstrate to God and to ourselves that we are serious about our relationship with Him. You show your seriousness by acting on His word, you can not fast filled with bitterness, anger and any other form of negativity and expect to see God's blessings follow, rather let your heart be pure, let go of all those that have trampled on you, let God minister peace in your heart so that your sacrifice may be holy unto Him.

Remember what Jesus said, "Mercy, not Sacrifice" Matthew 9:9-13. Be merciful to others and He will be merciful to you, then you can bring your sacrifice of fasting before Him. Well you might say, "Pastor Maria you're a joker, you want me to forgive my ex-husband or ex-wife? You want me to forgive my step-mother or step-father, no way" But listen to me my beloved, I felt the same way too after that fellow came into my ministry and disrupted everything, I struggled to forgive, I was so frustrated until God gave me the grace to forgive and even pray for those that had taken advantage of me. God has commanded us in His word in Luke 6:27-28:. "But I say to you who hear: Love your enemies, do good to those who hate you, bless those who curse you and pray for those who spitefully use you." May the Lord help you to understand the power of forgiveness so that your prayers may be answered, that is what true fasting means.

"For I desire mercy and not sacrifice, and the knowledge of God more than burnt offerings." Hosea 6:6

To paraphrase, He said that to love God and your neighbour is worth more than all the sacrifices and burnt offerings. In other words, **to love is better than having to say we're sorry.** To love is better than having to repent for doing something wrong.

To truly love is better than any offering or sacrifice, for it does away with the need to have to sacrifice and bring offerings, which proves it was never a requirement by God, but only a concession because of the hardness of people's hearts. Also, animal sacrifices became too easy since it is much easier to lay down the life of some animal than it is to lay down one's own life and do away with the sinful nature. So child of God understand this, true fasting is about your heart, it's about your obedience to God. Do what He says, love His people and serve Him with all your heart then your prayers will be heard.

Chapter Two

PRAYER

Prayer is communication between God and man. It is not meant to be a monologue, but a dialogue between God and man. Prayer is the vehicle that transports you from one spiritual realm to another. Listen my friend; according to Jeremiah 33:3 when you call on God, He will answer you, and show you great and mighty things, which you do not know. Paraphrased: He will open your eyes to see into the spiritual realm.

God's hand moves when the people pray. His desire is for us to communicate with Him, He is our Father. Can you imagine living with your father in the same house and not talking to Him or talking to Him only when you want something from Him? This is a rather sad situation because it is what most of us do. I wish we could get to a level where we understand that God loves us so much He desires our attention and fellowship with Him so that our bond with Him can be strengthened everyday.

John Wesley was a man of prayer and a friend of God, he daily communicated with Him, he recognized the power of prayer when he said, "Give me 100 preachers who fear nothing but sin and desire nothing but God and I care not a straw whether they be Clergy or laymen, such alone will shake the gates of hell and set up the Kingdom of Heaven on earth. God does nothing but answer to prayer." My dear, there's no short cut to miracles or breakthroughs, it is through prayer, prayer is the master key, why don't we get back to the place of prayer? We want to spend time socializing with friends and family but when it comes to spending time with God we take it for granted. It becomes a burden. Help us God! May the Lord open your eyes to understand the power of prayer child of God, may He give you the grace to pray, and as you keep seeking Him surely you will not fail in life but you will soar like an eagle and you will live to see the goodness of the Lord in the land of the living. Amen.

Prayer provides the Christian with the oxygen required for spiritual survival. Prayer brings us into fellowship with God the Father, Son and the Holy Spirit. This means that if we don't pray we will be lacking spiritual oxygen and we will end up struggling physically and spiritually. This is also because prayer brings life, joy, peace, and many other blessings. How can you expect the Holy Spirit to minister to you or even show you things in the spiritual realm about yourself and your family when you don't have a relationship with Him?

Prayer is Effective

"This is the confidence we have in approaching God: that if we ask anything according to His will, He hears us. And if we know that He hears us whatever we ask we know that we have what we asked of Him" (1 John 5:14-15).

Indeed prayer is very effective and extremely powerful as long as it is according to the will of the Father. The above scripture says He will answer. All you have to do is make sure you pray and fast with a right motive. You shouldn't see your sister with a posh car and rush into the presence of God with covetousness in your heart and expect Him to bless you, or beat on your wife and treat her like nothing and assume God will honour your prayers. It doesn't work that way.

The word "effective" comes from the word Effectual, energeo in the Greek language which means to be active, efficient. From Webster's dictionary, it means, producing or capable of producing an intended result or having a striking effect, able to accomplish a purpose; functioning effectively. Pray and believe that your prayers will bring results; your prayers are supposed to accomplish a purpose. When the devil attacked me by using someone to try to destroy our ministry I had to go into serious prayer with fasting. I pleaded with God to bring results, and in the end there were results. As God intervened, He delivered us and the entire church. As a result, there was restoration and deliverance. That is the effective prayer, when you see tangible results! My prayer produced results; by the grace of God it impacted the kingdom of God.

Pray in the name of Jesus, in the authority of His name, according to John 14:13-14 "And whatsoever ye shall ask in my name, that will I do, that the Father may be glorified in the Son. If ye shall ask anything in my name, I will do it" That's it, Jesus has given you authority, use it that the Father's name may be glorified in your life. "Don't be anxious about anything, but in everything, by prayer and petition, with thanksgiving, present your requests to God. And the peace of God, which transcends all understanding, will guard your hearts and your minds in Christ Jesus" (Philippians 4:6-7).

At one point I became so anxious when I realised that I believed the lies of that person concerning our ministry, for a short while I couldn't even pray, the spirit of confusion had attacked me and it was not until I became determined and said to myself, "Maria, get up and pray, greater is He that is in you than he that is in the world, don't fear" Then I started seeing my breakthrough unfold, I am forever grateful to the Holy Spirit who gave me the strength to pray and the victory.

When we pray we discern the will of our Father; effective fervent prayer seeks to find God's will and to make that will our prayer. Effective fervent prayer does not seek for deliverance as the priority but for God's will to be done. We become God centred and not need driven. I prayed for the will of the Father to manifest in my life and in the ministry, I sought God's face concerning what He wanted me to do in the Sunday school and in the end He revealed it to me.

Watch and pray, stop wasting your time. Remember you have the power of the

Holy Spirit who helps you to pray and reveal all things, He also affirms the perfect will of God for that which you are seeking. Use your heavenly language to travail, to speak to God and have Jesus intercede on your behalf to our Father; and wait for the answer. We cannot be limited by time or demand that God answer in our own time; we must be prepared to wait on Him for as long as it takes.

Chapter Three

CONSISTENT PRAYER

I have realised that many of us pray but we are never consistent in our prayer life. We need to be consistent in our prayer with fasting. Some Christians pray but when they don't see results they give up; they are not ready to wait, they are unreliable, they never turn up for nights of prayer yet they blame God and their leaders, accusing them of not praying for them. How do you expect God to answer you when you are a part time intercessor? Today we see you in church but the next time we see you is about a month later. It doesn't work that way, you need to pull your socks up and get serious with prayer; then will your deliverance come, along with your miracles and success in life.

Prayer delivers the oppressed, releases the afflicted and sets the captive free. Prayer opens the windows of heaven; prayer will break the limitations and set free the demon **possessed**. And I decree and declare to you that from today every bondage that has been holding you is being destroyed right now in Jesus' name, rise up and shine, for the glory of the Lord has risen over your life, rejoice child of God, don't fear, you have a weapon in your life, and that's the weapon of prayer. Use it to fight the enemy of your soul, don't grow weary, don't say, "Well Pastor Maria I have done everything and nothing is working." Hey sis or brother, don't give up! And don't confess negative. Someone said, "In consistency lies the power" so be consistent in everything, keep on praying, fasting, praising God, giving, do what God tells you to do and wait patiently, before you know it you will have your miracle in your hands, you will rejoice; weeping may endure for a night but your joy will come in the morning.

Prayers make insurmountable mountains surmountable. It makes the uncrossable river crossable. It moves obstacles. It divides the sea, makes us pass through the fire unaffected, it puts demons on the run, forces the roaring lion to tremble. It brings down the high wall of Jericho in our lives and this will be your portion in Jesus' name. From today your prayers are answered, obstacles in your life are bowing down before you in the name of Jesus. As you read this book, oh yes, receive the anointing that destroys yokes and removes burdens in Jesus' name.

Prayer turns failure to success and defeat to victory. It makes a way where there is no way and opens closed doors. By prayer, you can influence the future. You can change the very circumstances that surround your life. I mean you can re-write your destiny through intensive prayer. Wow! I love prayer! When I gave my life to the Lord that was the first grace that rested on me, I looked at my life and it was a mess. I remembered what they had spoken into my life, 'how I was not going to amount to anything in life; and I refused it. I entered into prayer and fasting, I travailed and wept before God, and started to decree what God had shown me about my destiny. I was consistent, I never gave up. Indeed our God is a faithful God, He answered and delivered me, He gave me a new beginning, a new chapter, a new destiny, and He turned my mess into a message. Friends, prayer with fasting works, it has worked for me, and it will work for you. It worked for Daniel and his friends in the Bible, and all the many other characters we read about in the Bible that God answered. So shall it be for you. God shows no personal favouritism to any man, He will remember you and bless you.

To be prayerful means to be more powerful and forceful over life's adversities. How well you know God largely depends on how much time you always spend in His presence praying, worshipping and beholding the glory in His Word. Give prayer a place in your daily life. A person who prays will always have domineering power over the diverse forces of life.

Deliverance

Consistent prayer brings deliverance. I have many testimonies of how I travailed in prayer until I saw God answer my prayers in many areas of my life. There are many things that consistent prayer does but let us look at the area of deliverance. Peter was in prison and Herod promised himself the great pleasure of putting him to death.

"The night before Herod was to bring him to trial, Peter was sleeping between two soldiers, bound with two chains, and sentries stood guard at the entrance. But the church was earnestly praying to God for him" Acts 12:4-5.

The walls of the prison were very thick, but prayers were offered without ceasing. It was consistent and unstoppable; there was no sleeping and no gospel artist to keep them fired up, but they prayed, they offered heaven bound prayer. The soldiers were very watchful. Theologians say there were sixteen of them, four squads of four soldiers each appointed to watch him in shifts of four at a time, and he was chained by both hands to two of them. Yet the church offered up prayers on his behalf without ceasing, the type of prayer that laughs at stone walls, handcuffs, iron bars, and gates of brass. **And so** in the middle of the night an angel struck Peter on the side, woke him up, and told him to get up quickly. And as Peter obeyed, the chains fell off of his wrists. Then the angel said to him, "Put on your clothes and sandals." And Peter did so. "Wrap your cloak around you and follow me," the angel told him. Every locked door opened by itself as he advanced, my God! What a mighty God we serve! He doesn't need any man's help; He is God by himself, the self-existent One. Wow!

In spite of his miserable circumstances and the prospect of being executed the next morning, Peter was sleeping so soundly that the angel had to strike him and lift him up. Even then, Peter still thought he was dreaming until the angel left him outside in the street, see Acts 12:10. I believe Peter slept with this scripture on his mind "He will not allow your foot to be moved; He who keeps you will not slumber." Psalm 121:3 Friends let us learn how to rest in God, He is the prince of Peace, ask Him to give you peace in this financial crisis. When the Home Office of Heaven is working on your status don't allow the devil to put you down, cast your cares on Jesus; He cares for you, in His time He will see you through. Don't lose your peace over your circumstance, I am not belittling your situation, but the truth is God is able to do anything for you as long as it is His will.

Peter found himself in the street, and wondered whether he was awake or seeing a vision. And when he got to the house where many people had gathered and were praying, they were all equally surprised, and thought it must be Peter's spirit, and that it could never be Peter himself. Yet there he was, in his flesh and blood, out of prison in answer to their prayers. This is my own belief, I believe some must have fasted, don't joke with prayer and fasting, demons had to bow down before the name of Jesus; they gave way for the man of God to be free.

And so in prayer there is deliverance, God's people pleaded for Peter. Don't give up on prayer, you will grow in your prayer life, don't worry even if you can only pray for ten minutes, it is better than nothing, keep on praying, determine to increase it to fifteen, then thirty, before you know it you will be praying for hours. That is how I started, it was not easy, it was a process, and today by the grace of God prayer is my life style.

I have heard testimonies of people that have been spared in answer to united prayer; many spirit-burdened believers have obtained gracious liberty through the prayers of the brothers and sisters. It is good practice to often lift others up to God in prayer, remembering those who are in prison for their faith in Christ, as if we were tied with them.

Chapter Four

CHALLENGE

In 2006, my Daughter backslid and got married to the father of her baby who is a Muslim. As a Pastor and leader, it was not an easy thing; it was a challenge to my faith. Before I received the message, in the early hours of that Sunday, at about 3.00 am, the Lord work me up and changed the message that I was to preach at the Sunday morning service to "Rejoice in the midst of the storm" as I was writing, it never occurred to me that God was giving me a message for the next phase of the challenge I was about to encounter. You must know that nothing takes God unaware; He is Omnipresent, Omniscient, and Omnipotent, so He gave me a word to prepare me. Whatever challenge or challenges you are going through God has already given you the grace to go through the fire and come forth without even the smell of smoke on you. Hallelujah!

That morning, I preached powerfully by the grace of God, and some members of the congregation wept. My daughter was not in Church that morning but she came to see me in the evening with the father of her baby, and that was when she disclosed what they had already done. There was nothing I could say or do at that time, but in my spirit I realized that the message I had preached in the morning was for me although it touched some of the congregation. Friends, my daughter was wearing an abaya, a long black garment worn by Muslim women, and I suddenly lost appetite. I felt like I was robbed of all that I had. When my daughter left, I went to my bedroom and rolled on the floor and cried, 'God what is all this? How am I going to handle this?' I was really crying out my heart in pain when I heard a word in my spirit, James 5:13: Is any one among you afflicted? Let him pray. At the same time, the message that I had preached earlier in the day echoed in my spirit. I immediately got up and addressed the devil, devil you will not have my daughter, you are a liar! I mentioned the situation to one of my leaders, and she responded, "Pastor Maria, this is not a good report, we must pray and snatch our daughter out." I said to my self, thank you Jesus, here is a mother who is feeling the pain I am feeling.

The following morning I called my fellow ministers and partners to stand with me in prayer, we decided on a dry fast to see the salvation of the Lord for my daughter.

I remember when I told my Pastor, Dr. Albert Odulele, he advised me and said, "Woman of God, I know it is not easy, but for you to win them you have to love them, meanwhile, we will be praying, and he concluded, you must pass this test." While all this happened, I went shopping with my daughter and those who knew me would look at me and look at my daughter with this question in their eyes: what happened? But they could not ask me, and I too would respond in my mind 'she is my daughter, I will not give up on her, she is coming out of that and she will live to serve Jesus.'

Beloved, from the time the incident took place I never stopped fasting with prayer, seeking God's divine intervention for my daughter's deliverance. She only spent two months in that relationship. One afternoon I was in the office when she called, "Mummy please can I come and see you?" I told her sure you can come, when she arrived she started crying, saying, "Mummy what have I done to myself? What happened to me? I can't believe this is me." She went on to say, "I woke up this morning and I felt I didn't love him any more." She saw one of my leaders in the office and she commented 'see she has the Glory of God all over her' and I told her not to worry because God was ready to restore her.

That afternoon, by the time she left my office, she had made up her mind like the prodigal son in the Bible to come back to God. I was so overwhelmed with joy, it was too much for me; God had leveled what looked like a big mountain, and in the twinkling of an eye the challenge was dealt with. God miraculously performed a quick miracle for me, He delivered my daughter and today she is serving God passionately. The devil was defeated, he was put to shame, indeed there's power in prayer with fasting, don't give up child of God, imagine if I had given up? Where would my daughter be today? I refused to listen to the devil's lies and I put my eyes on Jesus the author and finisher of my faith.

Chapter Five

HEARING GOD DURING FASTING

When fasting, it is so important to ask God to help you keep your mind on Him because the devil will try to distract you even more than usual because he knows that you are so determined to seek the face of God. The devil knows that fasting sharpens our hearing, and through it God exposes his plans, so he fights tooth and nail to resist you from hearing God's voice.

When I am on a fast I hear the voice of God more clearly and I have heard many of God's people testify to how fasting sharpened their receptivity to God's signals; it is almost like fine tuning a radio. When Jesus taught His disciples about their need for growing faith, He made it clear in Matthew 17:21 that prayer and fasting were important for a greater level of faith. Fasting is an aid to increasing faith when our motive is to draw closer to God so that we can hear Him better.

Let me make my self clear, when I talk about hearing God during a fast, I don't mean God only talks to us when we are fasting. No, God speaks to us at all times but when we fast, we hear Him better. As a child of God, hearing Him is vital to your walk with Him because you are supposed to be in a relationship with Him.

I mentioned earlier how fasting sensitizes your spirit in order to help you discover the perfect will of God for your life. It is a period of seeking His face for a particular reason, and He will speak to you through His word or in a vision. In Acts 10 Peter was fasting with praying on the rooftop when God gave him a new revelation and called him to take the gospel to the gentiles. Peter was able to receive this revelation because he was found in the place of prayer, and prayer along with fasting fosters spiritual sensitivity. But when we are too busy with every day activities and cares of life we just might miss Him.

"For it is not ye that speak, but the Spirit of your Father which speaketh in you."Matthew 10:20 (KJV)

God speaks by the Holy Spirit through His written Word, through His anointed servants, and through such supernatural means as dreams, visions, and inward assurance. God never speaks to us in any subjective experience contradictory to His written Word. So as you fast, read the word of God so that any idea or word that drops in your spirit can be cross checked with God's word.

Every experience must be judged by the Holy Scriptures. We need to open our hearts to receive the word of the Lord not only from the Bible, but through the other channels by which God speaks. Listen out for what the Holy Spirit is saying; stay there until He releases you. When God reveals something to you by insight, and gives you a conviction, you are moving beyond the simple text into the Spirit realm. For example; God shows you the plans of the devil or shows you some things about your future. These revelations are God's ways of showing His affection for us. In case you are having a challenge hearing God's voice, I recommend that you read the book titled "Understanding God's Voice." It was written by my mentor, Dr. Albert Odulele, and it will help you tremendously.

The bible says, "Be still, and know that I am God…'" Psalm 46:10 KJV

It's in the place of silence that the Holy Spirit picks apart the truth we receive from scripture down to its essence, reveals specific insights that are pertinent, and then applies them to our most perplexing problems and stubborn misconceptions. As He transforms our heart to beat in sync with His, our decisions begin to accomplish His will and we begin to reflect His character. Try it. Open the Word of God in a peaceful place and sit in quietness before Him. In time, the Holy Spirit will illuminate a passage and it will come to life in your mind. Before you know it, the knotty situation that drove you to distraction will unravel. You will clearly know His will, and direction in life.

God is not withholding from us, trying to confuse us or laugh at us as we strain to hear His voice. If we find ourselves having a tough time, it might be that He is encouraging us to press in a little closer or tune into a new frequency. But be assured He wants you to hear Him.

Deuteronomy 29:29 says, "The secret things belong unto the Lord our God: but those things which are revealed belong unto us and to our children for ever, that we may do all the words of this law." God does not withhold from us He actually wants to reveal His great and unsearchable things to us.

As we pray and fast, God isn't the only one who speaks, the devil does as well, and he is the reason we sometimes miss it. But I am forever grateful that all things work together for good for those who love God and are called by Him. So many times we make mistakes but when we go back to Him and repent, He is always willing to forgive us. He turns our mistakes into a stepping stone; don't allow your mistakes to stop you from going forward. Don't be afraid of failure: When we face failure, sometimes the biggest lesson we can learn is that we CAN keep going. You might fail, but if you don't keep trying you'll never succeed. I am reminded of the story of Thomas Edison and all the failed attempts he made when inventing the light bulb. When asked why he kept trying after so many failures, his answer showed that after each failed attempt, he saw things from a different perspective. He never saw those failed attempts as mistakes; he felt that each one eliminated a solution that wasn't right. He was learning much from each so called mistake. We can too. Edison used his mistakes as stepping stones; he never allowed his mistakes to deter him, and in the end, he was able to come to the right solution that brought about the light bulb. You can do the same thing he did; you can use every mistake as a stepping stone to your destination at the top

Making a mistake as it regards hearing God's voice can be costly for every one of us. Though, very often, afterward, we can see more clearly how we went astray. There was a sister who badly wanted to get married; she prayed and fasted, but she was already determined in her heart to marry this brother she was dating. I do not know how she expected God to show her Mr. Right when she had already made up her mind to go with this guy? She went ahead and married the guy, today they are divorced. She put words in God's mouth by telling her pastors God had told her to marry this guy. What a pity? Please if you are waiting to hear the voice of God, close your ears to your own voice and the devil's and ask the Holy Spirit to take over. Many of God's children have neglected the place of prayer and the study of God's Word; the two practices that are supposed to enable them to hear God clearly. Regardless of all this, most seasoned believers have some mystery mistakes. In other words, everything seemed to indicate God was saying one thing but something entirely different came out. I have more than a few of those myself. But so what? God is working everything out for good in our lives, even the mistakes we make when it comes to hearing him. And how do we know what the ultimate outcome will be? That's for us to find out eventually as we trust Him in faith, but until then it's not over till it's over, like Pastor Mathew Ashimolowo says.

The truth is that we can't always avoid mistakes when it comes to hearing God's voice but that is not the end of the world. What does the scripture say?

"For a just man falleth seven times, and riseth up again: but the wicked shall fall into mischief." KJV Proverbs 24:16

Though you have gone through temptations that assail your mind, and afflictions that press down your body, as you repent and ask God's forgiveness you will emerge; and as you pass through the furnace, you will come out brighter and more refined. Listen to what the scripture says, but the wicked shall fall into mischief and there they shall lie; having no one to uphold them. My beloved, I believe everyone has made mistakes of failing to hear the voice of God in one way or the other so get up and seek the face of God once again, and this time, be careful.

If you think you have heard something from God, seek Godly counsel; submit that to those with spiritual authority over you and see what they think. After the trauma I went through in our church, I made up my mind that I will never embark on any project, or make any major decision before praying and seeking the counsel of my spiritual father and mentors.

After seeking their counsel, ask yourself, "Does their counsel confirm what I have heard?" If those around you are troubled, a red flag should go up; God isn't going to give opposing answers to the same question, therefore something must be wrong; stop and pray some more to discover if that someone is you.

If you feel rushed and pressed about a certain matter, it probably isn't coming from God. Be patient. Have you noticed how slow God often seems? We want to hear NOW! But He has His timing and a plan. Take the necessary time to pray and seek direction and advice before acting on what you believe is God's voice.

Chapter Six

THE KEY TO OPEN HEAVEN.

Fasting with prayer is the key to open heavens, we see this very clearly in Deuteronomy 28:23: And your heavens which are over your head shall be bronze, and the earth which is under you shall be iron. The book of Deuteronomy 28 talks about blessings and curses. What causes a person to walk in the blessings is their obedience to God's instructions, which is His word, while curses come as a result of disobedience to the word of God. Having a dedicated time of prayer and fasting is not a way of manipulating God into doing what you desire. Rather, *it is simply forcing yourself to focus and rely on God for the strength, provision, and the wisdom you need.* Although I am talking quite a bit about open heavens, I am in no way advocating that your focus should be on getting your prayers answered, even though that is important, it is more important to have a good motive when you go in prayer with fasting, your aim should be relating with your Father, praising and appreciating Him after which you make your requests known before him.

In 2004, upon realizing that certain things were happening in my life that ought not to, I decided to set my heart on the Lord and to seek Him through payer with fasting. On the last day, I laid still in His presence to hear from Him and I suddenly heard clearly in my spirit, "You are now walking under open heaven." I was shocked, because at that time I had been a believer for 10 years, serving God diligently only to find out that up until then, I had been walking under closed heaven! I pondered within me about the number of people out there who have been born again for years but still walk under closed heavens without realizing it, simply because they spoke in tongues and quoted the scriptures? Oops! God help us! What God revealed to me humbled me that day and it still does today. That is why it is very important for you as individuals to seek God in prayer with fasting for ourselves. Friends, this is about destiny, there are levels God wants to take you to and it will take determination to conquer the Goliath that is mocking you and your God. It can be an accusing voice in the spiritual realm from your father's house that does not want you to amount to anything, they may have set a limitation over your life. You must take your position in the spirit and declare no more limit, there are household wickedness that are trying their best to see that you don't fulfil destiny, fight against it like a wounded lion. Don't grow weary, the people that know their God shall be strong and carry out great exploits, stand and fight in prayer with fasting.

The Bible says in Psalms138:8 "The Lord will perfect that which concerns me; your mercy, O Lord, endures forever; do not forsake the works of your hands." God is a merciful God. According to the scriptures He cannot forsake you because you are the work of His hands. Once you have the right key you will be able to open the door, fasting with prayer is one of the keys that opens heaven.

Obedience

Whenever God is going to give you a miracle He will first give you an instruction, if you obey the instruction then you will receive the miracle. After fasting or in the midst of fasting, God can give you an instruction and it is your choice to obey or disobey. Disobedience is like the sin of witchcraft, it displeases God; if we fail to obey Him it will hinder our blessings. What has God told you to do brethren? Are you willing to obey? Or are you going to live a life of rebellion? It's up to you to make up your mind today and say to yourself, "enough of not paying my tithes, enough of not honouring my parents, I am going to follow God's command." Don't bother fasting if you are not ready to do the will of God; if you are walking in waywardness.

Obedience is something we teach our children to do and something we expect others to follow. We expect people to obey the laws of the road, for example; when we are driving on a narrow street, we are told to give priority to on coming cars, so we expect the other driver to wait. We expect people to be quiet during the movie, so those who are being loud are deemed as rude and inconsiderate.

There's an unspoken rule between friends, and that is that we often listen and act on each other's suggestions in order to demonstrate our love and acceptance of each other; thus, solidifying the friendship. So why is it so hard to obey God? Are His rules so hard to follow? I personally have learnt that through His grace and the power of the Holy Spirit we are able to live holy lives that are pleasing to God. Allow the Holy Spirit to guide you in obedience; He is always talking to our inner man.

Are you willing to listen? Are you ready to please Jesus the lover of your soul?

His will

Spending time in prayer with fasting is not automatically effective in accomplishing our desires; it will not open the heavens unless we do things according to His will. Fasting or no fasting, God only promises to answer our prayers when we ask according to His will. 1 John 5:14-15 tells us, "This is the confidence we have in approaching God: that if we ask anything according to His will, He hears us. And if we know that He hears us - whatever we ask - we know that we have what we asked of Him." In the prophet Isaiah's time, the people grumbled that they had fasted, yet God did not answer in the way they wanted, according to Isaiah 58:3-4. Isaiah responded by proclaiming that the external show of fasting and prayer without the proper heart attitude was futile, Isaiah 58:5-9. So for you to get good results from God you have to walk in obedience, you have to do the will of the Father.

How can you know if you are praying and fasting according to God's will? Are you praying and fasting for things that honour and glorify God? Does the Word clearly reveal that it is God's will for you? If we are asking for something that is not honouring God or not God's will for our lives, God will not give us what we ask for, whether we fast or not. How can we know God's will? God promises to give us wisdom when we ask. James 1:5 tells us, "If any of you lacks wisdom, he should ask God, who gives generously to all without finding fault, and it will be given to him." Listen to me and listen to me carefully, your heaven will open on the condition that you forgive, stop tearing down your leaders, end strife, stop thinking you are more important than every body else. Humble yourself before God, acknowledge your weaknesses and failures and God will exalt you in due season.

Chapter Seven

DURATION OF FASTING

There are many types of fasting, pray about the kind of fast you should undertake. Jesus implied that all of His followers should fast (Matthew 6:16-18; 9:14, 15). For Him it was a matter of when believers would fast, not if they would do it. Before you fast, ask God the type of fast He wants you to undertake; is it a dry fast? Is it water only, or water and juices; what kinds of juices will you drink and how often. Restrict some activities because you need to concentrate and be devoted to prayer and God's Word.

Let us look at the types and Duration of Fasting

1.   Supernatural Fast – Moses – (40 days)

2.   Emergency Fast – Esther – (3 days)

3.   Consecrated fast – Daniel - (7-21 days)

1. Supernatural fast

Moses fasted 40 days – Exodus 34:28 - KJV "And he was there with the Lord forty days and forty nights; he did neither eat bread, nor drink water. And he wrote upon the tables the words of the covenant, the Ten Commandments."

If you have never fasted before I welcome you to this journey, it pays off, see how God visited Moses? He can do it for you as well, I will not lie to you by telling you it is easy; but you can do all things through Christ who strengthens you. The fact that you are holding this book shows that you are interested in fasting; I applaud your present interest! Fasting takes the grace of God; you might be struggling but yield to the Holy Spirit. Fasting has been a major emphasis in the lives of many of the great spiritual leaders throughout history. John Wesley, the founder of the Methodist denomination, fasted every Wednesday and Friday and required all of his clergy to do the same. Effective ministers of God from the apostle Paul to Martin Luther to John Calvin made it a continual part of their walks with God.

None of those men had a "formula fast" that was the only "right" way. Fasting is about the condition of the heart, not the number of days. Each time that I have fasted for forty days, it was because I felt impressed by God to do so. Be led by the Lord, that's the best fasting you can do. Start slowly; fast one meal a day, or one day a week, or one week a month. Build up your spiritual muscles so that you will be prepared in a period of several months to fast for an extended 40 day period. God can lead you to fast at night; in this case you will be awake the whole night praying and not eating or drinking or as God tells you.

When it comes to making your final decision about what type of fast is right for you, the best advice I can give you is to follow the leading of the Holy Spirit. He will guide your heart and mind as to what is best for you. Please be careful as you fast, if you are on medication please consult your doctor, use wisdom; don't just cut out on eating but be led. If you are pregnant or nursing you may be exempt from a fast, as may be moderately ill people. If one is otherwise healthy but has a headache and finds it difficult to fast, he or she may eat, but you can fast another time.

Remember, the most important consideration in fasting is your motive; why are you fasting? To seek something personally from God's hand or to seek His face in worship, praise and thanksgiving.

2. Emergency Fast – Esther – (3 days)

Esther agreed to intervene with the king on behalf of her people. She earnestly sought God in prayer at this critical juncture and indeed God intervened. Esther was also looking for the support of the Jewish community by asking them to join in this fast.

All in all, as you fast, make sure you release people; pray for your enemies and bless them, don't say, after all Esther fasted with the Jew and Haman was hanged, No! It doesn't work that way, the Bible says, 'Bless those who curse you, pray for those who mistreat you.' Luke 6:28 NIV .

Real forgiveness means praying for them to be blessed! Are you serious? Totally! Real forgiveness is hard because it goes against how you might feel, nobody else might ever know that we forgave the offence, it's tough to see God answer our prayers by blessing the one who hurt us as though they never did one thing wrong. Keep yourself holy whether fasting or not, don't fast and start quarrelling or gossiping, that's not fasting, or else your prayers will bounce back to you.

3. Consecrated fast

Daniel fasted 21 days –
(Daniel 9:3-4,Chronicles 10:12)

What is consecration? According to the Easton's Bible Dictionary, consecration is the devoting or setting apart of anything to the worship or service of God. The Israelites devoted their fields and cattle, and sometimes the spoils of war, to the Lord, Leviticus 27:28, 29. God wants you to be devoted to Him fully; as you fast, switch off your TV, cell phone, lap top, and set your self apart for God.

The word, Consecration, is an Old Testament word meaning to devote, separate and dedicate or set apart for the service of the most High God. So as I said, we have to set ourselves apart for the service of God, separate your selves from your friends, colleagues and family and seek the face of

God. I don't mean abandon your job or spouse, no! Use wisdom; before you go into fasting, if you are married, speak to your spouse so that you can be in agreement because a house divided cannot stand.

Consecration means yielding your will to God, it means the presentation of ourselves to Christ for His glory, beloved, yield yourself to God, give your life to God fully so that His glory will be revealed in you. Let your fasting be acceptable in the eyes of God, see to it that your heart is clear, get rid of envy, strife, and all other negativity otherwise you are simply wasting your time fasting to closed heavens.

Child of God, like Daniel fasted, you too can do a partial fast and have a successful fasting experience. I have seen some Christian men and women choosing the Daniel fast as their guideline to enter into the spiritual discipline and God has answered their prayers because they fasted as they were led. While the Daniel fast is a partial fast, rather than total abstinence from all food, it provides many of the attributes of denying the self and seeking God. No wonder Daniel came out of the lions' den vindicated and without so much as a bite mark, it's because he was a man of prayer, a man who fasted and prayed. Ruth, a young widow, found Boaz, the love of her life, and married him. They experienced rejection and hardship, yet they succeeded in what God had called them to do because of prayer and I believe fasting as well.

I gave my heart to the Lord Jesus in 1994 at the Abundant Life Ministries where Rev Chigbundu was ministering during a night vigil. I had been invited by my hair dresser on the previous Saturday and it was my first time at a Pentecostal church. Coming from a Catholic background, everything was strange to me; the worship, the prayer, as a matter of fact I was confused. I was raised by my aunt to fear the Lord but when I came to England I did not practise that. Unfortunately, that night, the pastor did not call an alter call, but when I left the service I knew the Lord had touched me. I knew this because during the worship I did not know a single song, but when I quietly asked the Lord to teach me how to worship Him, suddenly a light shown on me and I started singing with every one. Friends, I left that service different; I felt as light as a feather, and when I got home I started to look for my Bible, I found it on top of a cupboard full of dust, and from that moment on I could not stop reading it; I was full of joy unspeakable.. I couldn't wait for the next Friday to come because it was announced that

Rev. Chigbundu was ministering at the Abundant Life Ministries in Peckham the following Friday. It was very cold, and because I did not know my way, I had to take a taxi with my daughter.

The message he preached about curses was an eye opener. I told myself; 'Lord, this is the moment to give you my all.' That day I gave my life to the Lord Jesus. Everything seemed to be happening so fast, I was on fire for God, all those who knew me could see the transformation, and even my daughter noticed the change, one time she said to me "Mum thank God you are born-again because you don't shout at me anymore." Friends, I am being real, when you don't have Jesus you will take your frustrations out on your children, or your spouse. Through my daughter's comment I learnt that when someone is frustrated they tend to take it out on others.

Four weeks after my conversion I felt a conviction in my heart to go on a seven day consecration fast, I said to my self 'I have never fasted this long, how is this going to be?' I could not shake it off; the amazing thing is that this was not coming from my mind but from my heart. I went and told one of the brethren what the Lord hard laid on my heart. Oh my God! That was the worst mistake I had ever made, the person crushed my spirit. There are certain things that God will tell you that are to be kept between you and Him so watch out, don't go telling people or your staff, they just might discourage you. I went back to God and asked Him again to confirm to me if I should really go on this fast. I remember it was at the 'Mission to London' 2004 meeting, that evening, Pastor Benny Hinn was ministering, and the power of God was so tangible I found myself weeping and telling the Lord 'here I am take my life and use it for your glory, whatever you tell me I will do.' The same word came again; "go on a seven days dry fast" although I had just spoken to the Lord about giving all to Him, suddenly there was a battle with my flesh. I knew without a shadow of a doubt that I was about to embark on a new journey with the Lord. God being so faithful, while we were still in the service, Mrs Esther Ayigbe tapped my shoulder and said, "Anena it is important to be obedient to the Lord when He speaks." At that point I told her how the Lord was calling me to go on a fast; her response was 'He who is calling you to fast will give you the strength to go through it because the call of God is upon your life.' From that moment on, I made up my mind to fast, I asked the Holy Spirit to give me the strength. God gave me instructions on my assignment, and since then I have also grown to love the Lord more until this day.

Jesus fasted for 40 days.

Jesus, our perfect example, fasted; He waited upon His Father, Why? He needed spiritual renewal and guidance, and the fellowship of His Father. Just like Jesus, we need to fast to get guidance from God, to keep our spiritual antennas sharp, to get the healing power of God, to gain wisdom for the resolution of problems, and for a special grace to handle difficult situations. Please make it a habit before you go on any fast to ask the Holy Spirit to clarify His leading and objectives for the prayer and fasting. This will enable you to pray more specifically and strategically.

We talk about "imitating Christ," but we only want to imitate whatever He did that fits our tastes. Jesus fasted, He went through trials; you too will face temptations as you fast, but stand. Can you imagine what it must have felt like after Jesus fasted 40 days; He was hungry and Satan offered to satisfy His hunger in a perverted way: '...command that these stones be made bread' (Matthew 4:3 KJV). One of the hardest things to do is say no when you have a legitimate need that can be satisfied in an illegitimate way. But Jesus stood, He never gave in to the devil, you too must stand; don't give in to the devil's evil plans.

The six types of fast found in the Scriptures are:

1. The Absolute Fast: This should be done only for a very short period of time. It is total abstinence from food and water. Only for a short period of time, the person observing the fasting with prayer does not eat any food, vegetables, fruits, nor drink water for the number of days he or she chooses.

2. The Normal Fast: On this type of fast, you typically go without food for a certain number of days but you drink cold or warm water and plenty of it depending on the length of fast. You may also choose to take clear broth and juice in order to maintain your strength.

3. The Individual Fast–(Daniel 9:3; Matt 16:18)– You don't need to tell anybody about it. Once you advertise it you have already got your reward. (Matt 6:1-4). Jesus concluded and said "Your Father who sees in secret will Himself reward you openly."

   Jesus was talking about public and private ministry.

4. The Partial fast – This fast can be interpreted in many ways. It usually involves giving up

a particular type of food and drink for a certain period of time. The person going for this kind of fasting with prayer may eat once or twice per day, and eat very little in each meal, the eating is not for satisfaction, and they deny themselves of their normal diet and eat reduced rations. It also involves giving up a particular type of food and drink for a certain period of time, like Daniel and his three companions did. You can even fast your favourite programme on television. During the time that the programme is on you will be before the Lord in prayer or in the Word of God.

a. You don't eat any food, fruit or vegetables but you can drink water. Water stands to be the major thing to take during this type of fasting with prayer.

b. Fruit: During fasting with prayer fruits will be the main thing to be eaten. All manner of fruits can be eaten during the fast with prayer.

One time, as I was watching a television program titled "Sunset Beach". I realized that I was being drawn into it, so I purposed that every time this programme aired I would go into my prayer room and worship

God. I felt relieved and happy because it was becoming an idol before God. I believe you are saying, "Yeah right!" But my friend, this could probably have been a trap from the devil, please understand me, I don't mean the program is a devil but I mean if you can not leave your program to go into prayer then something is wrong. I would encourage you to surrender your program to God for a certain period of time, and God will be so pleased with you.

5. The Corporate Fast – Isaiah 58: This is for the body of Christ to seek God together. Usually, everyone is fasting for the same period of time and same purpose.

In the beginning of his captivity in Babylon, Daniel and his three companions refused to eat the choice meats and sweets from the kings table, asking instead to have only vegetables and water.

Chapter Eight

GUIDELINES TO FASTING

There is a need to be prepared before we go into fasting with prayers. For us to succeed in anything we do in life there must be preparation. Prepare before you go into fasting by checking your heart and making sure it is right with God and man.

And Samuel spake unto all the house of Israel, saying, if ye do return unto the LORD with all your hearts, then put away the strange gods and Ashtaroth from among you, and prepare your hearts unto the LORD, and serve him only: and he will deliver you out of the hand of the Philistinies. 1 Samuel 7:3

Set within you the numbers of days you are going to hold the fasting with prayer, with the purpose. I remember 12 years ago when the Lord pressed in my heart strongly to go on a fast, I purposed in my heart to go for 3 days dry. On the third day when

I was concluding, I realized that the Lord had not spoken, I told myself but the Lord has not spoken. So I poured the tea in the sink and I told the Lord, 'You haven't spoken!' so I pressed in for the forth day. On the fifth day I had a visitation that changed my life and launched me to a new dimension in God.

You set the time and period when to break. These are the things you are going to commit to God in prayer. I know that God knows everything; He is Omnipotent, Omnipresent and Omniscient. All these are true but you have to tell Him what you are about to do if you want Him to be part of the prayer with fasting.

Let's see what God told the Israelites after they had fasted for a whole period of seventy years.

"Speak unto all the people of the land, and to the priests, saying, When ye fasted and mourned in the fifth and seventh month, even those seventy years, did ye at all fast unto me, even to me?" Zechariah 7:5.

God knows that they were fasting but they were not fasting in the right and proper way, and they did not inform Him before they started the fast.

"Now in the fourth year of King Darius it came to pass that the word of the LORD came to Zechariah, on the fourth day of the ninth month, Chislev, ² when the people[a] sent Sherezer,[b] with Regem-Melech and his men, to the house of God,[c] to pray before the LORD, ³ and to ask the priests who were in the house of the LORD of hosts, and the prophets, saying, "Should I weep in the fifth month and fast as I have done for so many years?" Zechariah 1:3 NKJV

This was a rhetorical question. The fact that they asked it indicated that these fasts were a burden to them. The truth is the Lord had never commanded them in the first place. They had fasted for a long time but it was all in vain, may that never be your portion in Jesus' name. Always be led, don't go according to what you feel but listen to that still voice in you. You may fast for 100 days and God is not aware that you are fasting or that you fasted at all. Listen to want Paul says, 'Be careful for nothing; but in everything by prayer and supplication with thanksgiving let your requests be made known unto God.' Philippians 4:6

When we fast, either corporately or individually, it would be good to observe the following guidelines.

1. As I said earlier, formerly proclaim the fast before God and dedicate it to Him. Ask for His strength and help during the fast so that you can complete it successfully.

"That thou appear not unto men to fast, but unto thy Father which is in secret: and thy Father, which seeth in secret, shall reward thee openly. Matthew 6: 18 KJV

2. Decide the purpose of the fast (i.e. the reward you expect from the fast) There should always be a reason for fasting. It can be some specific desire (e.g. the salvation or deliverance of men). It can be just for general spiritual exercise and fellowship with God. This type should be done regularly for example, . weekly and forth nightly etc. but not too long; as fasting brings you closer to God.

3. Prepare yourself and dedicate that fast to God (Proverbs 3:6). Whenever you are on a fast, remember, if it doesn't mean anything to you, it will not mean anything to God. Without combining it with prayer and the

Word, fasting is nothing more than dieting or hunger strike.

4. Examine yourself, if you find any sin in your life, repent and turn away from it. Open your heart before God. (Psalm 139:23-24)

5. Ask yourself "What is the purpose of my fast?"

6. Be expectant.

7. Spend time meditating on the Word of God as declared in Joshua 1:8, and in worship and prayers.

"This book of the law shall not depart out of thy mouth; but thou shalt meditate therein day and night, that thou mayest observe to do according to all that is written therein: for then thou shalt make thy way prosperous, and then thou shalt have good success. Have not I commanded thee? Be strong and of a good courage; be not afraid, neither be thou dismayed: for the LORD thy God is with thee whithersoever thou goest." Joshua 1:8 KJV

Fasting puts you in a place to hear the voice of God; it sensitizes your spirit and helps you understand the mind of God for yourself. Fasting does not change God but it changes you and conforms you to the word in obedience. You must keep your mind on

God when you are on a fast and any feelings of hunger are reminders for you to get in the Word of God and the place of prayer; plan to be authentic or your fast will fail. When the fast is authentic, that means it is being done properly, you do what is required in the fast and set yourself aside.

Child of God, if you don't do according to what is required in the fast it will not produce the required results. Whatever you do during the fast will increase; if you are seeking God's move, it will increase. If you are praying it will increase.

Fasting should change your life and make you want more of God. Fasting is feeding the hungry and being conscious of the things of God; so when it is done, it looses the bands of wickedness that are assigned against you. A fast that is not authentic is the fast that does not produce the type of results the Bible talks about in Isaiah 58:3-5.

Chapter Nine

BENEFIT OF FASTING

Fasting can be so challenging but I want to assure you that it has physical benefits that you will experience and will cause you to be so grateful that you obeyed the voice of God. Believe it or not, I don't want to lie to you that when God calls me to fast I throw a party or rejoice, no way! It hits me because I love to snack, I enjoy food; especially chapatti, it is so delicious. Chapatti is unleavened flat bread (also known as roti) from the Indian subcontinent. Versions of it are found in Turkmenistan, in East African countries like Uganda, Kenya, Tanzania, and in some parts of West Africa like Ghana.

There are times when I am preparing "Mr. President's" dinner, this is my five year old grandson's nick name, and I usually feel so tempted to eat, even if it is just a little, but I ask the Holy Spirit to give me the grace to persevere. Parents can understand where I am coming from or those whose profession is in the food industry. But once I remember the importance of obeying God and its benefits, I take my stand, and really the results are phenomenal.

The importance of fasting within the body of Christ *cannot* be underestimated.

I have heard (and I also teach) that we should be led of the Lord in our fasting. All Christians, but especially those who fast, should keep themselves in the Word of God as well.

First of all, you must know that when you go on a fast, you are giving your body a rest to remove pollution and toxin, Since fasting is a period of partial or total abstinence from food and other physical activities in order to seek God, it causes the power that should have been used to perform those activities to be diverted into prayer, and this makes our prayers more effective and more powerful, and increases our ability to hear or receive from God more accurately. Proverbs 14:30a "A sound heart is the life of the flesh..." in other words fasting keeps you sensitive to His spirit and causes you to live holy because fasting subdues the outer man and brings the inner man alive.

Doctors today are discovering the physical benefits of this practice and have found that abstaining from food (not water) for several days has a wonderful cleansing effect upon the body. Many impurities are burned up within the body as it is denied food, thus clearing the mind, and cleansing and healing the body. Even nature shows us that fasting is good medicine since we automatically lose our appetites when sickness strikes. Many people in the world are practicing fasting and finding it is not only healthy, but it is also a wonderful way to lose weight quickly. However, even though we may enjoy these benefits while fasting, the Christian primarily fasts for spiritual purposes and not for health reasons. Obeying spiritual principles can produce positive physical results, but they are added blessings. Even people that are underweight who fast for spiritual purposes have been known to gain weight after completing their fasts.

Fasting is a constant means of renewing your spiritual walk with God, I call it spiritual service, if cars are serviced ever so often to make sure they are in good condition how much more we Christians?

We renew our spiritual strength through fasting with prayers, Isaiah 40:31 it says "But they that wait upon the Lord shall renew their strength; they shall mount up with wings as eagles; they shall run, and not be weary; and they shall walk, and not faint." During a fast, God strengthens and renews you and sharpens your vision so that you can run the race of your divine assignment. You must know that all of us here on earth were created with a purpose in the creator's mind. Just in case you are having a challenge discovering your assignment, I would like to recommend a book titled "Divine Assignment Indicators" by my Spiritual father, Dr. Albert Odulele. The book is a real blessing and it will give you clarity on your divine assignment.

Fasting prepares you for a new anointing, Psalms 92:10 "But my horn shalt thou exalt like the horn of a unicorn: I shall be anointed with fresh oil." I have come to understand that in every new level in God, there are new devils, therefore you cannot operate on yesterday's or last year's anointing and revelation; you need a fresh anointing and that will not come by eating three square meal a day. As we fast with prayer and study the Word, we experience a new measure of the anointing of God. God fed His people with fresh manna everyday and the same happens to us when we wait on Him; He gives us fresh revelations, instructions and directions. Good health and healing spring forth after fasting.

In Isaiah 58:8 the bible says, "then shall thy light break forth as the morning, and thine health shall spring forth speedily: and thy righteousness shall go before thee; the glory of the Lord shalt be thy reward KJV

I remember five years ago, when for no apparent reason at all I started experiencing pain in my back; I said to myself this is strange, I have not lifted anything that would cause this. Based on the above scripture, I decided to fast and I spoke to my body, saying, "this is the temple of the Holy Ghost, you pain go back to where you came from" and by the third day the pain had left.

Through fasting with serious prayers, we deal with the enemy of our soul and stand our ground for our destiny. Fasting breaks poverty from your life. Isaiah 58:11 narrates, "And the Lord shall guide thee continually, and satisfy thy soul in draught, and make fat thy bones, and thou shalt be like a watered garden, and like a spring of water, whose waters fall not." Also, fasting will overcome sexual addictions and demonic powers. There are curses that will be destroyed from your life as you fast with prayers. I realized that because we are in Christ we tend to think that the enemy can not attack us, and when he strikes we don't seem to understand what is really happening in our lives, but as we seek God's face in fasting with prayer there will be deliverance and you will see the salvation of the Lord.

I mentioned earlier about my daughter and how she backslid from the faith, there was nothing I could do but fast and pray. During that period, for two months I did not touch any food but drank only, crying out to the Lord to restore my daughter; and He did. So fasting with prayer will cause God to bring back your son or daughter from the prison cells; it will deliver them from fornication and every other type of negativity out there. May be you are reading this book now and your children are hooked on drugs or they have left home and they won't even listen to your voice, please love them; fast and pray because God promised to save us along with our household.

As you fast with prayers, God rewards you openly in such a way that when the answer comes all eyes will see and testify of the goodness of the Lord by saying, "this is the doing of the Lord and it is marvellous in my eyes" that is the way I am testifying now. *Hebrews11:6 "But without faith it is impossible to please him; for he that commeth to God must believe that he is, and that he is a rewarder of them that diligently seek him." (KJV)* There are great benefits in fasting with prayer so let it be part of your life style because there may be certain spiritual forces that have oppressed your family for years and you must rise up like Deborah and Gideon to throw down those demonic alters. It will take your determination.

Queen Esther called her people to a three day fast; no food or water, before she went in to see the King. I'm sure they prayed for her personal protection as well as favour with the King for the lives of all the Jews. The amazing result of that fast is now history. You see, when you fast, God grants you favour such that the people from whom you never expected favour will begin to favour you. I have seen God favour me and I wonder why, sometimes I break down in tears and ask my self, "Maria do you deserve all this?" Indeed friends, no one makes a sacrifice to separate himself or herself to seek God only for God to put them to shame.

The Lord tells us in **Matthew 6:16-18** that *when* we fast, we are to do it unto the Lord. He doesn't say *if* we fast see below:

"Moreover when ye fast, be not, as the hypocrites, of a sad countenance: for they disfigure their faces, that they may appear unto men to fast. Verily I say unto you, They have their reward. But thou, when thou fastest, anoint thine head, and wash thy face; That thou appear not unto men to fast, but unto thy Father which is in secret: and thy Father, which seeth in secret, shall reward thee openly."
Matthew 6:16-18 KJV

We can see that our motives for fasting must be pure. We are not to do it as a show off but as quietly and simply as possible so that we do not attract attention to ourselves. Remember, when you fast you are pleasing God, and that is a powerful benefit. Do you know what it means to please God? It means to obey, worship, and pray to him. And when you please Him, He will cause your enemies to be at peace with you, according to Proverbs 16:9.

Fasting builds our faith. In fact, this is what Jesus meant when He spoke to the disciples in Matthew 17:21 when they were unable to cast a demon out of a child. He said, "Howbeit this kind goeth not out but by prayer and fasting." He was telling them that if they wanted to get their faith to the level of casting out that type of demon, they needed to fast and pray for their faith to increase.

So child of God, with all the benefits we have looked at, I believe your life will never remain the same so go forth and pray with fasting, and God's deliverance, protection, and many other benefits will follow you, I could never exhaust the list but I feel led to share these ones.

Chapter Ten

"WAITING" - ISAIAH 40: 28-31

Fasting and prayer is a form of waiting on the Lord for strength, fresh oil, times of refreshing and renewal, as in Isaiah 40: 31 KJV "But they that wait upon The Lord shall renew their strength; they shall mount up with wings as eagles; they shall run and not be weary; and they shall walk and not faint." There will not be freshness without waiting, and without waiting there will not be renewal. So in order to mount up to a new horizon you have to be willing to wait to be renewed in order to mount up.

What is waiting?
The Hebrew Word to wait means to "bind together, tangible entwine or tarry expectantly as a waiter at a restaurant waiting to serve. When we bind ourselves together, God's presence will begin to rub on us. If you bind yourself to God, waiting on Him, you entwine yourself, you become stronger in Him and you become a stronger vessel unto Him.

Waiting on God allows you to tarry. When you tarry it has to be with expectation that is what praying with fasting is all about. Don't give up on waiting on God for Mr. Right or Ms. Right, give me a second before you doubt what I am saying, indeed no one who waits on God will ever be ashamed but those who deal treacherously will be ashamed, Psalms 25:3. When you run out of patience you will lose trust in Him. If you do not wait on God you will end up in danger.

Waiting on God requires concentration, it requires the quiet hour of prayer and meditation when we put aside the interests which occupy us in our everyday life and try to relish God's presence. Let's make out time to be quiet in the presence of God so that He can lead and instruct us, and help us to walk in His foot steps.

Renew

Let's look at the word "renew". In Hebrew, it means "to change". Literally, "renew" means "exchange." When you trust in God who is omniscient and omnipotent for your supply of order, intelligence and power, He will exchange your weakness and foolishness for His strength and wisdom. What a deal!

When you are entwined with God it changes your life; your old nature is transformed into the new nature of Christ. You change from a position of weakness to strength, from failure to success, from fear to boldness, from disappointment to appointment, from rejection to acceptance, from poverty to riches, from mess to message. Dearly beloved, look at this verse in Ephesians 1:6 "...He made us accepted in the Beloved" You have a new family, you are not alone, the entire host of heavens is watching over you.

As you wait upon the Lord, He will renew your strength; His anointing makes the wounded and weary rise again with renewed energy and purpose. And I pray that such will be your portion. Maybe you've experienced a tragedy that has left you feeling indifferent about the future, or a heartbreak that has you still feeling pain; there's hope for you, God's strength is available for you and He will renew yours.

Remember the Bible talks about being transformed by the renewing of your mind, Romans 12:2. How will your mind be renewed? This happens in the presence of the Lord; there He meets you and changes your mind and thinking as you study His word.

But waiting isn't always inactive; sometimes it's active; like waiting on your pastor and seeing that his or her needs are met. Waiting isn't really a posture, it's a focus. Isaiah says, 'Thou wilt keep him in perfect peace, whose mind is stayed (focused) on Thee…' Isaiah 26:3. Whether it's sitting prayerfully in God's presence, or actively carrying out His will, you've got His assurance that your strength will be renewed.

Pay close attention to the following promises; the Psalmist says, "Wait on the Lord; Be of good courage, And He shall strengthen your heart; Wait, I say, on the Lord!' Psalm 27:14, '…wait silently for God alone, For my expectation is from Him' Psalm 62:5 '…as the eyes of servants look to the hand of their masters…So our eyes look to the Lord our God…' Psalm 123:2.

Before I gave my life to the Lord. I remember how I used to fear people. It was so bad, I couldn't just talk to people, but as soon as I got born again, the fire of the Holy Spirit came upon me and I could go to the streets and tell people about the love of Jesus. I remember once meeting a Muslim man on the bus, after I handed him a leaflet, he looked at me with such sternness; if this had happened before I gave my life to the Lord, I would have been shaking like a leaf. On this occasion, the man was trying to convert me to the Muslim faith by telling me Jesus was just a Prophet and I was in the wrong faith, but I responded, 'NO, I AM NOT, Jesus is the son of the living God, He came to redeem mankind. That is the love of the Father; He loved you even though you didn't know Him and that is why He has sent me to speak to you.' Before we could continue he stepped off the bus.

Those who knew me before I gave my heart to the Lord are still amazed at what God has done with me. So as we wait upon the Lord His nature rubs off on us and we become more like Him, He empowers us, the Spirit of boldness rests upon us and before we know it we are doing exploits for Him.

Do people see a change in your life? Are you afraid of their faces? God told Jeremiah 1:8 "Be not afraid of their faces: for I am with thee to deliver thee, saith The Lord." This also applies to you, be strong don't be intimidated by people look up to God; He is on your side.

Not only do the scriptures say we wait upon the Lord, they also say we shall 'mount up.' Let us find out what it means.

Mount up

In Hebrew and Greek, this occurs when you are in a place and are catapulted up. To mount up means to increase, develop, produce, be fruitful. God desires that you mount up with confidence and assurance. .It also means to lift up; many of God's people have been down and depressed but God has sent me to tell you that from today onward you are going to mount up like an eagle. If you have been in a place in your life where there is no mounting up going on, you must know that mounting up comes only as you wait on God and are renewed. When I talk about mounting up, what comes to my mind is the eagle. Let us take a look at this unique bird; I am sure there is a lot to be learnt from it.

Isaiah 40:31 "....they shall mount with wings as eagles, they shall run and not be weary, and they shall walk and not faint."

What is an eagle? An eagle is a large bird of prey, it is a member of the bird family accipitridae, and it belongs to several genera which are not all closely related. The eagle is born with its mouth wide open. Its nest is found ruffled because it is born to fly. It is a bird of tremendous character and possesses supernatural strength. It is blessed with sublime vision. It is not without its own enemies, it can fly in the midst of a storm, it mates for life and returns to the same nest, and it goes through the moulting process of renewal.

The eagle is the most majestic bird in the sky. However, something happens to all eagles at least once in their lifetime – they moult. In the life of every eagle, they will go through a moulting process that can bring with it a great depression. This is a wilderness time that all eagles go through. Certain eagles live for 30 years or more but at some point, they begin to lose their feathers and their beak and claws begin to change. Experts tell us that during this time the eagle will walk like a turkey and will be without the strength to fly. There it remains in the valley, unable to fly, with its feathers falling out. It loses its ability to see as well as it used to because its vision weakens during this time, calcium builds up on it beak so that it cannot hold its head up. This is quite a traumatic experience for this proud majestic bird. It loses its desire to eat (eagles are carnivores by nature) and has no strength to hunt.

Another phenomenon takes place: when the moulting eagle gets in this last state, often times it will begin to peck on another moulting eagle that is sharing a nest with it, occasionally killing it. At this time it will choose a spot on a mountain range where the sun can shine directly on it while it sun bathes on a rock. During this time, it has been said that other eagles come and drop food for the moulting eagle, however, it is never the younger eagles that do this, it is always the older ones who have survived this experience and know what the moulting eagle is going through.

Wow! I find this quite interesting and begin to think that, if eagles support each other like this; shouldn't we children of God do more for one another? There is a problem in the body of Christ; it breaks my heart when I see saints tearing and rejoicing over other believers going through a time of trials. I do not mean to say that all believers do this, but it is quite unfortunate that it does happen in the church. I went through this as well; I shared a little about it in the earlier chapters. After all that I went through I was attacked left right and centre by some believers in the body of Christ who laughed at me and mocked me. It's sad that some of them never understood the whole scenario of what I was dealing with, and yet they decided to be judgemental. I have even heard stories of believers who have left their churches because of fellow brothers and sisters in the Lord that back stabbed them. Let this be a learning experience for us all.

One expert writes about the following scenario "…it is a most pathetic sight to see". Four or five eagles moulting in the valley, where they once would only soar over to look for fresh kill, but if they don't renew, they will die, the moulting eagle will grow weaker and weaker. And then a sound from the sky over the valley, of another group of screaming eagles who drop fresh meat over the moulting birds. Experts say the screaming is an encouragement from other eagles that have already gone through this. Some eat and recover but others roll over and die. Henceforth when you see your sister or brother suffering; call them, cheer them up, visit them and speak kind words to them, avoid judging or blaming them.

In the previous chapters, I mentioned what I went through with my daughter. While I was fasting, the Holy Spirit spoke to me saying "…the trial you are going through is going to make you strong and help you identify with other people that are in the valley so that you may bring encouragement to them."

Jesus said something profound in Luke 22:3. He said, "Simon, Simon, behold Satan hath desired to have you, that he may sift you as wheat. But I have prayed for thee, that thy faith fail not: and when thou art converted, strengthen thy brethren."

You must know that Satan is in constant desire to have you so that he may sift you as wheat from your destiny. In order to fulfil destiny there has to be focus. Without focus there is no fulfilment of destiny. While the eagle is going through its trials, it is focused, that is why it is able to win in the end. No matter what trials you may be going through dear readers, stay focused on Christ, there is a future and a hope for you; the expectation of the righteous can never be cut short.

According to the text in Verse 32, Jesus, who is our intercessor, is in prayer for you that your faith fail not, and when you are converted strengthen thy brethren.

As Christians, we are in the army of The Lord, 2 Timothy 2:3, "thou therefore, endure hardness as a good soldier of Jesus Christ." As a soldier in the army of the Lord we cannot rely on our own strength. It is not by might nor by power but by the Spirit of God.

The eagles possess supernatural strength; you also have the strength of God as long as you rely on the Holy Spirit at all times in order to soar above the storms of life. As stated above, the eagle is not without its enemies. The enemy of the eagle is the snake, and most of the time it creeps into the nest to eat the eggs and the eaglets. In my study, I found out that the eagle, because of its sublime vision, will spot the snake and swoop down to pick it up and soar very high with it only to drop the snake on the rock. When the snack lands on the rock it is crushed to pieces.

Child of God, for you to know the wiles of the devil you have to always have a good relationship with God, He will expose all his evil plans, he will cause you to spot the enemy, the devil.

Sometimes in our walk with God, we know that our hearts deceive us. For example, many of us have been in church a long time and do not appear to recognise when Satan crawls into our territory, simply because we have become familiar with God and our vision has become dim. It is only after we have been bitten that we wake up. I realised that nursing the wound and drawing out the poison that has been injected in your spiritual life will cost you more than you think. So from time to time we need to go back to God in prayer with fasting to sharpen our vision and direction.

Chapter Eleven

LEARNING FROM THE EAGLE

One morning, as I woke up to pray, I felt the Lord telling me that there are many things we can learn from the eagle. I started meditating on it and what I discovered was amazing. Let us set aside what we looked at in the previous chapter. An eagle is a huge bird with a white head and long yellow claws which swoops down on a river and snatches a fish right out of the water. It's an impressive sight to see. The eagle is perceived as a symbol of courage and power. The Hebrew word for eagle is nesher, meaning "to tear with the beak." The eagle tears with its beak when its in hiding, this teaches us that when we are fasting and praying we are in a secret place with the Lord; here He deals with our character, we get transformed into the nature of Christ and we become very potent in your lives.

Secret place

One distinctive characteristic of the eagle that holds well is that they never flock as the vultures do. This experience can be related to us; during prayer and fasting, one needs to enter into the secret place of the Most High, it is a time to separate your self from people, from your busy schedules and wait upon the Lord. Learn from the unique eagle, why spend your time hanging around people that are not taking you any where? Turn off that TV, computer, black berry, iphone and have fellowship with your God. Technology has become an idol for some believers, please understand me, I am not against any of the things I have mentioned but you need to strike a balance in your life, Dr. Josephine Kyambadde says, "put an end to the busy schedules and people that have been drawing you away from God and seek His wisdom…time management and prioritizing is so important if we are to live a balanced life." I highly recommend this book that was written by my mentor, it has blessed me so much and it is titled "The Balanced woman" it is not for women only; men, this book will help you too. In her book, Dr. Josephine Kyambadde teaches us how to use our time wisely by setting time aside for fellowship with God and our families and for every other important thing in our lives.

Eagles select the tallest trees of the forest, the topmost crag of the mountain, they live in solitude, hunting and feeding singly, whenever possible carrying their prey to the nest so that the young may gain strength and experience by tearing at it and feeding themselves. Prayer and fasting take us into the deep things of God; this reminds me of the scripture below;

"Deep calls unto deep at the noise of Your waterfalls; All Your waves and billows have gone over me." Psalm 42:7 (New King James Version)

This is the time you go deep in God with all the storms around you, when waves are breaking all over you, trying to tear you away from Jesus, the Rock to which you cling, and in which you have a resting-place. "All thy waves and thy billows are gone over me;" you are then whelmed in the deep, and God alone can save you, strengthen you and cause you to triumph.

As you get deep in His presence, your spirit will be tuned into Him, and you will be able to clearly hear God's voice; you will get spiritually fed and this will make you strong so that when the attacks of the enemy come you will be able to soar past them, and you will be well equipped for victory.

Protection

I want to refer to Exodus 19:4, it says, "Ye have seen what I did unto the Egyptians, and how I bare you on eagles' wings, and brought you unto myself." This "bare you on eagles wings" must not be interpreted to mean that an eagle ever carried anything on its back. It merely means that by the strength of its powerful wings it can carry quite a load with its feet; this is actually the natural way the eagles carries anything. The significance of this revelation about the eagle in relation to prayer and fasting is the power that is available to us during this spiritual exercise; knowing that our God will bare us up in His hands, lest we dash our foot against a stone, as in Psalm 91: 12. I have seen God's hands upon my life He has always preserved me from evil. There was a time when I was in prayer with fasting and I went to church, as I was getting out of my car another driver came by, driving so fast he missed me by just about an inch; he almost ran me over.

In Deut 32:11 we learn a very valuable lesson about how God allows us to go through adversities and

challenges so that we can come out in maturity...
."As an eagle that stirreth up her nest, That fluttereth over her young, He spread abroad his wings, he took them, He bare them on his pinions." Indeed, God in this scripture reveals Himself as the eagle who builds in us the tenacity to face our adversities. As you continue in the presence of God, He will preserve you from evil; you will not die a premature death but Jehovah God your protector will go all the way for you. He will not put you to shame, He will surround you with His angels, and the same God who preserved me from that car accident will do the same for you in Jesus' name.

Seeing in the spirit

"Does the eagle mount up at your command, And make its nest on high? On the rock it dwells and resides, On the crag of the rock and the stronghold. From there it spies out the prey; Its eyes observe from afar. Its young ones suck up blood; And where the slain are, there it is." Job 39:27-30 NKJV

The eagle is said to have such keen eyesight that even when she is so high in the air that men cannot see her, she can discern a small fish in the water! This is a sign of watchfulness and vigilance; dear brother and sister, watch and pray; be vigilant, the devil is like the roaring lion looking for someone to devour.

This is what happens; when we get closer to God, He opens our spiritual eyes so that we are able to discern the ways of the devil or see the great and unsearchable things of God, Jeremiah 33:3. Right now God is giving you the eye of an eagle and you will be able to see spiritual things from afar, you will be focused and your vision will be strong and clear; there will be no confusion as He shows you visions and dreams. If you know that God has been giving you insights but the enemy has always made you forget or brought confusion, believe and receive that it will never be the case for you again as you continue to seek Him.

Back to the eagle, the eagle will stay on a cliff, dwell and make her home; this is a sign of Great habitation. Let God's presence become your habitation, not the shopping mall or clubs.

Did you notice that the scripture says, 'Her young ones also suck up blood' this is a deep sense for generational maintenance and successful planning. Be a good planner; plan your life wisely, never rush out of your house without talking to Jesus the King of peace or else you will always live a stressful life; this world is full of stress and pressure, evil news is all around us, that's why you need to be prepared and equipped with God's word so that you will not be blown away by the storms of this life.

When you fast and prayer with the right motive you will see victory in your life, failure will never be your portion.

Renew our strength

Psalm 103:5 is a reference to the long life of the eagle. The bird has been known to live to an astonishing age in captivity; under natural conditions, the age it attains can only be guessed. "Who satisfieth thy desire with good things, So that thy youth is renewed like the eagle." This reveals longevity when we live a holy life. I believe by now you are saying, Pastor Maria, 'I have seen people who lived holy and died young', yes you are right, the scriptures tell us that "For My thoughts are not your thoughts, nor are your ways My ways, says the Lord. For as the heavens are higher than the earth, so are My ways higher than your ways and My thoughts than your thoughts." Isaiah 55:8-9. Beloved, God knows what He is doing; we can never question Him, we will only understand some of His decisions when we get to heaven. But all in all, as you wait upon God He will renew your strength, you will not grow weary, in serving Him, loving others, giving and helping as it is needed.. .

Sometime back while I was studying the eagle, I saw this verse Proverbs 30:19: "The way of an eagle in the air; The way of a serpent upon a rock: The way of a ship in the midst of the sea; And the way of a man with a maiden." This reference to the eagle is to that wonderful power of flight that enables a bird to hang as if frozen in the sky for long periods appearing to us as fixed or its ability to sail and soar directly into the eye of the sun, seeming to rejoice in its strength of flight and to exult in the security and freedom of the upper air.

"He giveth power to the faint; and to them that have no might he increaseth strength. Even the youths shall faint and be weary, and the young men shall utterly fall: But they that wait upon the LORD shall renew their strength; they shall mount up with wings as eagles; they shall run, and not be weary; and they shall walk, and not faint." Isaiah 40:29 –31 KJV

This scripture refers to the eagle's power of flight. When you fast and pray, you are lifted into a higher dimension and a deeper frequency.

Have you ever become weary in your Christian walk? Oh! Come on; don't act as if you are the Virgin Mary! Every body has been there before. There have been times when I felt that I just couldn't go any further because of the trials.

As I reflect on those times, I realize that the reason for my weariness was that I was operating in my own strength. I was trying to live a Christian life by my own strength, not the strength that God gives. This scripture clearly teaches that no matter how strong and vigorous we are in the natural, if we rely upon our own strength, we will get weary. Remember the time when Elijah was running away from King Ahab and Queen Jezebel. He fled to the desert and collapsed under a Juniper tree. Twice, as he lay there, an angel came and woke him and provided food and water for the weary prophet. There the Angel of the Lord spoke to him, "Arise, eat, because the journey is too great for you." (1 Kings 19:7) After eating the food that the Lord had provided, he "went in the strength of that food for forty days and forty nights to Horeb, the mountain of God." (1 Kings 19:8)

I have come to understand that the journey that God has called us to is too great for us. I have realized that I am not strong enough, brave enough, or wise enough to accomplish the work that God has appointed for me. If left to me, I would certainly fail and fall short of all that God has called me to be and to do. My only hope is to receive strength and nourishment from the Lord. Only by exchanging my weakness for His strength can I walk this Christian life.

What then, is the secret to receiving the Lord's strength? We must "wait on the Lord." God is not talking about some kind of passive resignation. We are not just to sit back idly, hoping that someday God may decide to answer our prayers. Instead, we are supposed to be in an active state of watching, hoping, and expecting for God to answer us. The Hebrew word for wait literally means "to bind together." We must bind our hope and expectation to the Lord. The Lord is not just our plan "A", while we keep plan "B" just in case He does not answer us. God is our only hope and expectation. Without

Him, we have no other option. We have no plan "B". We need
Him and His strength.

Chapter Twelve

MORE LESSONS ON THE EAGLE

The Overtaking anointing

"Their horses also are swifter than leopards, And more fierce than evening wolves.

Their chargers charge ahead; their cavalry comes from afar; they fly as the eagle that hastens to eat." Habakkuk 1:8 NKJV

This reference uncovers the swiftness of the flight of the eagle; and it reveals an overtaking anointing that we get when we pray and fast and an increased level of sharpness and sensitivity in the spirit. May the over taking anointing rest on your life from this day onward so that you can overtake those who are ahead of you. Amen.

Friend, do you know that because I have made prayer with fasting, and relying on God's grace my life style God has promoted me so much that I look at my life and wonder, how it all came to be for an orphan like me! I now sit with people of high profile, God has divinely connected me to greatness, and the people that I don't know are serving God together with me. I wake up and take some time to decide what to wear because of the many clothes that God has given me, and by the way I don't buy them, God sends people who shop for me from shoes to jewellery, etc. When I decide to go to any country, I simply get up and go, and I stand up to speak before multitudes. That is what I call the overtaking anointing. There are some people who used to put me down, laugh at me, criticize my dress code because of the financial challenges I was facing, at one point they told me, "why don't you close the church? God is not with you; after all you have only a few members." I know I had heard from God from the secret place of thunder so I could not heed their advice. I am here to encourage you; hold on to whatever God has spoken to you. There IS a reward in waiting. My God has promoted, elevated and set me apart! Hallelujah! Come on! Rejoice with me friend! Blessed be the name of the Lord. I have a story to tell, I remember how I suffered when I was young; I suffered from rejection, when my parents had a motor accident, according to my culture, my uncle was supposed to take custody of me but his wife rejected me and my auntie Epifania stepped in and told the elders, "If you don't want to look after her I will take her."My father had three wives, so the rest of the other children had their mothers to take care of them so they were alright, but I wasn't, and because of that I will always be grateful to God that He used my auntie to care for me and teach me the fear of God. I am who I am today because God used her to lay the foundation of my destiny.

It is God that has exalted me from nothing to something and this is just the beginning, the world has not yet seen what my God is going to do in my life. Eyes have not seen, ears of men have not heard, and the hearts of men have not yet perceived what my DAD is going to do in my life. I am not bragging, I am sharing what my God has done, with all humility. The Bible allows us to boast, as long as it is in our God. The angels of God overcame Satan by the blood and the word of their testimony.

For you too, your season has come, your weeping is over, God has heard your prayers, they have come before Him as a memorial, its time for you to dance, laugh, and shout with shouts of Joy! Apostle Paul said,

Romans 8:18 "For I consider that the sufferings of this present time are not worthy to be compared with the glory which shall be revealed in us."

What God has prepared for you, I am talking about His glory, is far greater than the pain, disgrace, disappointments, confusion, fear and rejection you may have gone through. Your enemies will see His glory on your life; they will get the shock of their lives. After God has performed the miracle, go and testify, let your enemies hear what the Lord has done. Don't allow the enemy, Satan, to whisper in your ears that 'you are showing off!' No Way! You are not showing off! You are fluffing scriptures. Remember, the angels overcame Satan by the blood and by the word of their testimony. When the devil whispers that jargon in my ears I always tell him to get lost! Don't mind him, enjoy your life, celebrate yourself, you have cried for years why not share the goodness of the Lord?

The enemy

The enemy of the eagle is the serpent and it crawls through the cracks to the nest for the eggs and the eaglets. Do you know that the devil is after that which God has birthed in you to ensure that there is nothing left of you? This could be in the form of a vision that has to do with your assignment in life and that is why you must have a sharp discernment to spot his operations.

I mentioned earlier about how I experienced such a dark period of my life that I suddenly found myself in the valley, and it was not pleasant. I didn't have the desire to eat physical food nor the Word of God but it really was the time I needed more of the Word of God than ever before. You look at life, and it is vanity upon vanity, as it is written in the Book of Ecclesiastes. This valley or wilderness experience is a very challenging period, so challenging that your emotion and feelings begin to talk to you. The enemy, Satan, speaks to your mind and this makes you weak in your body. Child of God let me tell you one annoying thing, you will not always be on the mountain top, soaring in the heavens, praying seven hours or casting out demons, no! There are grey days when you will be attacked and you will find it hard to pray, fast or even read God's word but I want to encourage you that, that is the time you refuse that discouraging spirit, call your pastor, friends, intercessors and share with them, let them pray for you so that the good Lord will bring deliverance in the end.

In the life of an eagle is noted that, in the process of moulting, the eagle's vision declines, that sublime vision that could spot a rabbit a mile away is lost. I want you to understand friend, when you are going through the valley experience, the enemy wants to cloud your vision with what you are going through. You know if you lose your vision in God, you lose everything. Proverbs 29:18 says, "Were there is no vision the people perish: but he that keepeth the law, happy is he." The devil is after your vision, don't give in; fight the good fight like Apostle Paul did. We are in a battle and we refuse to surrender to the evil one, we are more than conquerors through Christ who strengthens us.

Back to the valley I was talking about, the other day, someone called my office for an appointment after the ministration. I scheduled the appointment and the person came to see me and said, "God has sent me to help you with the Vision of the Children's Ministry." I was very excited and I thought that this was an answered prayer because I had been praying about this issue. To be honest, I was overtaken with excitement and I never sought God concerning this brethren looking behind, I was busy with the church and other projects on my plate. Friends, it was the greatest mistake I have ever made in my life. The enemy sent this person to destroy the vision and to scatter the work that God has entrusted to me. That is how I ended up in the valley for months crying to God to restore what the enemy had stolen from me.

Why did I not seek God's counsel before giving this person the children's ministry? Why did I not call my spiritual father for guidance? We learn by mistake, my beloved, before you make any move in life always pray first, don't be deceived by the outside appearance or by the eloquence of speech, no way! The devil is so cunning he never comes in form of a beast; he knows you will spot him, and therefore he will disguise himself.

I remember a pastor friend called and warned me to be careful, with that person" but I ignored the advice. Why didn't I remember this scripture Proverbs 11:14 "But in the multitude of counsellors there is safety." Because I didn't consult God before acting, why rush into that relationship? Have you prayed? Have you informed your parents, pastors or spiritual elders? Think twice before you act!

There are some people that are infested with deceiving demonic presences to abort visions and dreams, and they are sent your way to kill, steal and destroy you, be careful, watch out for them not everything that glitters is gold. Some of these wicked people look very intelligent, seemingly humble and suitable but these are wolves in sheep's clothing. They pretend to be the angel of light.

Friends, don't just get excited – guard that which God has birthed in you and through you with Godly jealousy. Remember that not everyone will celebrate with you when you run with the heavenly vision! Protect the Vision and do not lose focus! The only way to keep the vision alive and effective is to wait in the presence of God in prayer with fasting so that you have sharp discernment like the eagle in order to spot and crush the head of the serpent and all his agents.

The scripture in Hebrew 12:2 declares that we need to "...looking unto Jesus the author and finisher of our Faith; who for the joy that was set before Him endured the Cross despising the shame, and is set down at the right hand of The Throne of God.

Jesus is our Victory and delight. Child of God, it does not matter where you are right now.

Turn your eyes upon Jesus. Look fully in His wonderful face and the evil assigned against you shall be destroyed by the Lord's Glory and Grace.

Chapter Thirteen

MISCONCEPTIONS ABOUT FASTING

Some years ago our church was called to a 40 days corporate fast and during that time there were many misconceptions from some Christians about the length of the fast. Among which were, "are Christians supposed to fast since Jesus finished the work on the cross? And is it advisable to fast in today's world as a Christian? One common misconception that stood out was that fasting somehow "twists" the arm of God to do our bidding. I believe on the contrary, that when we fast, instead of us demanding that God do our will, we will have a greater sense and desire to do His will.

Does fasting move the hand of God? No. If we believe that God withholds from us and we have to fight to get Him to bless us, then we have a wrong conception of the Lord. Isaiah 58:6 indicates that fasting is not to move the hand of the Lord, but it is to make Satan turn loose that which he is holding back that rightfully belongs to us. Jesus died so we could have the blessings. They belong to us as God's children. However, we must press in and demand of the enemy to release what he stole from us. This is our right as sons of God. Sometimes Satan controls a large territory in our lives and in the lives of our loved ones. He's got many in bondage. Fasting is a key that breaks loose the bands of wickedness. As we fast and pray, Satan must let our teenagers who are bound by the spirits of rebellion and drugs go free. He must take his hands off our loved ones, our friends and family. Some people are so bound that only fasting can loose them from the wicked chains of darkness.

I once read a funny story that I cannot quite remember its source. One night, a few co-workers at the computer data centre were working late, and after sometime they all became hungry. They decided to order food by phone, but their boss thought that since they worked with computers, it would be more appropriate to order by internet. After they contacted a fast food chain on the web site and spent a long time registering as new customers for the delivery service, a message appeared on the screen: "Thank you for your business. You will be able to order food in three days." I laughed! In my heart I though to myself, it is probable that some of these people were Christians who were meant to be fasting for three days and some how got carried away and ordered food and that was a red light for them, if I had been part of the group I would have just given up, repented and gone back into fasting.

It should be noted that fasting is no substitute for obedience to the Lord in all other areas of our lives. We (in our modern society) are always looking for a microwave "formula" that will bring about the blessing. God knows our hearts, and He is just as concerned with what we are doing in other areas of our lives. This can lead to discouragement for some, who believe that fasting takes the place of obedience. Take a look at what the Lord said to Isaiah. The people were astonished that they were fasting and yet not seeing the desired results. God cuts right to the heart of the matter:

"Wherefore have we fasted, say they, and thou seest not? wherefore have we afflicted our soul, and thou takest no knowledge? Behold, in the day of your fast ye find pleasure, and exact all your labours. Behold, ye fast for strife and debate, and to smite with the fist of wickedness: ye shall

not fast as ye do this day, to make your voice to be heard on high. Is it such a fast that I have chosen? a day for a man to afflict his soul? is it to bow down his head as a bulrush, and to spread sackcloth and ashes under him? wilt thou call this a fast, and an acceptable day to the LORD? Is not this the fast that I have chosen? to loose the bands of wickedness, to undo the heavy burdens, and to let the oppressed go free, and that ye break every yoke? Isaiah 58:-6 NKJ

The fast that honours God not only includes abstinence from food, but a loving heart towards God and His people! So fasting is part of our Christian walk. The key to fasting has nearly been lost to the modern church. It is also one that some say was only for early day Christians. Looking closely at the Word of God, we find that the Lord never did away with the principle of fasting, but it has been man who has attempted to make it obsolete. Fasting is still a valid key that can be used today to bring us into kingdom living.

Fasting is a wonderful tool that has been given to help bring us into the presence of God and that is why the devil is bringing all his misconceptions so that we miss out on God's blessings. God's ultimate desire is that we live "fasted" lives, thus reducing the need for periodic fasting. However, until we come to the place where the kingdom of God means more to us than food, we need to set our wills to fast in order to bring our bodies under subjection to the Spirit of the Lord.

Paul was an overcomer, and he said in I Corinthians 9:27, "But I keep under my body, and bring it into subjection: lest that by any means, when I have preached to others, I myself should be a castaway." For us to overcome we must do likewise. To grow in God we must follow the methods He mapped out in His Word. The Lord is encouraging us to walk in His footsteps so that we might attain the same victory that Paul did. It is not impossible; we just have not understood God's ultimate purpose for our lives; we have lived far below the level God intended. Even though we might have to walk through some hard places in this life, at the end we will be able to say it was worth it all when we eventually come into the same place that Paul did.

2 Corinthians 11:27, "In weariness and painfulness, in watching often, in hunger and thirst, in fastings often, in cold and nakedness," Philippians 3:8, "Yea doubtless, and I count all things but loss for the Excellency of the knowledge of Christ Jesus

my Lord: for whom I have suffered the loss of all things, and do count them but dung, that I may win Christ."

Chapter Fourteen

PROPHETIC DECLARATION

I have disciplined myself to prophecy in my own life because the world we are living in today is full of negative people and negative news. We need to rise in prophetic proclamations and declarations to refuse the negative report of the enemy. We need to rise in the area of authority, moving in the power of God who is resident within us; calling into being the will of God for situations and circumstances; speaking into existence that which does not exist. During the fasting times your spiritual senses are greatly activated to become sensitive and discern the times. Like Ezekiel, God releases you to prophesy.

"The hand of the LORD was upon me, and carried me out in the spirit of the LORD, and set me down in the midst of the valley which was full of bones, And caused me to pass by them round about: and, behold, there were very many in the open valley; and, lo, they were very dry. And he said unto me, Son of man, can these bones live? And I

answered, O Lord GOD, thou knowest. Again he said unto me, Prophesy upon these bones, and say unto them, O ye dry bones, hear the word of the LORD. Thus saith the Lord GOD unto these bones; Behold, I will cause breath to enter into you, and ye shall live: And I will lay sinews upon you, and will bring up flesh upon you, and cover you with skin, and put breath in you, and ye shall live; and ye shall know that I am the LORD. So I prophesied as I was commanded: and as I prophesied, there was a noise, and behold a shaking, and the bones came together, bone to his bone." Ezekiel 37: 1- 7 KJV

Fasting brings us to the place of "bargaining grace" to decree a thing and cause it to happen in Jesus name. You will also declare a thing, And it will be established for you; So light will shine on your ways. Job 22:28. When you get into the secret place of the Most High God there's enough grace for you to decree and to declare, use this time to speak into situations and circumstances that you want God to change.

Ezekiel was authorized to prophesy unto the dry bones, an indication of our dry situation, and activate heaven for an intervention. Prophetically declare to yourself "I am coming out of this! I will not die! Devil you will not kill me! I have a destiny to fulfil!" Remember you are in a challenging situation, in a valley, you need to speak or else you will die spiritually. Proverb 18:20 says, A man's belly shall be satisfied with the fruit of his mouth; and with the increase of his lips shall he be filled.

Today, God continues to use prophetic acts and declarations to fulfil His will on earth. I heard a man of God (whose name I cannot now recall) give this testimony, "In 1990, one of the generation's spiritual influences, Cindy Jacobs, received a word from one of her friends who had been divinely instructed in a dream to bury the Word of God under the soil of Russia. Following the instructions of that dream, an evangelistic tract named "The four spiritual laws" was buried in the neighbouring soil of a university in Russia. After that, Cindy began to prophesy and proclaim words of victorious evangelism. "The seed from this tract will grow schools of evangelism, and theology will be taught", were her bold and confident declarations. At that time, the likelihood of that prophesy being realised was far from the people's imagination. However, after the fall of Russian Communism, evangelist Billy Graham started schools of evangelism on Russian grounds, thus fulfilling the words in Jacob's prophesy." This is the power of prophesying, keep on declaring what you want to see fulfilled in your life.

Dear reader, we are reminded in this scripture that, "Death and life are in the power of the tongue: and they that love it shall eat the fruit thereof." Proverb 18:21. My prayer for you is, you will take your position as a child of God and speak with authority into your situation and in the eyes of your enemy Satan. Refuse to remain where you are, greater is He that is in you than he that is in the world.

Prophetically begin to declare where you are going or where you want to be in life, especially if you don't like where you are. The Bible says we are the "People of Prophecy." You must know that when you are on a fast you become so strong spiritually, even though physically you may be feeling weak. You become more powerful, a weapon for God to use, remember you are His battle axe and with you God is going to shake nations.

With your mouth declare that:

"My God is a Great and Mighty God in whom I put my trust."

"My God reigns over every situation in my life."

"My God gives me His strength when I am weak."

"My God will stop every weapon that is formed against me."

"My God is my refuge and strength in the time of need."

"My God wants to prosper me and not harm me."

"My God wants to give me a hope and a future."

"My God hides me under the shadow of His wings.

"My God is my healer and my Peace.

"But they that wait upon The Lord shall renew their strength they shall mount up with wings as eagles; they shall run and not be weary and they shall walk, and not faint." Isaiah 40:31:

When the eagle is in the moulting stage, calcium builds up on its beak and it finds itself looking down, the eagle begins to help itself. They scratch at their own claws until the claws are down to nothing and as they are coming out the new growth appear. Some eagles will not be content to sit and die they will do something to help themselves. You need to learn from the eagle instead of sitting in despair, distress and confusion, do something about it, speak the word of God, prophecy into your situation; the spoken Word of God is what brings results. You have all that it takes to help yourself come out of where you are. Speak The Word; see yourself coming out, renew your mind by studying the word, listening to teachings and preaching on the word.

"So then faith cometh by hearing, and hearing by the Word of God." Romans: 10:17

"So shall My Word be that goeth forth out of My Mouth; it shall not return unto me void, but it shall accomplish that which I please and it shall prosper in the thing which I sent it." Isaiah 55:11.

If we make the effort God will respond to it. The Bible says "Say to them, 'As I live,' says the Lord, 'just as you have spoken in My hearing, so I will do to you: Numbers 14:28. Sitting about moping and weeping is not the thing to do but as with the eagle, the greatest thing the eagle does for itself while it is in this state of moulting is choosing a spot where the sun can shine directly on it. The eagle finds a rock and lays on it. It sun bathes and, lets the sun beam down on it; it simply waits there until it is renewed. Make a habit of listening to the Word of God again and again so that you may be renewed.

It is interesting that in the midst of the eagle's weakness it finds a rock, lays on that rock and lets the rays of the sun bathe him. Jesus is the Rock of Ages, the One we rest upon. He is the Sun who gives us strength as we wait on Him. His strength restores us. You must know that there will be a time in your life when you will need God more than you have ever needed anything or anyone, but don't just treat Him like a fire extinguisher that you only turn to when you need it! He loves you so much; He wants to enter into a relationship with you. He loves you so much it hurts. The humiliation and pain He suffered on The Cross proves that He wants to be part of you and I want to encourage you right now to let Him in and let yourself become all that He wants you to be.

If you do not know Him, pray this prayer:

Dear Heavenly Father I come to you in the name of Jesus Christ, your word says "…whoever comes to me I will never drive away." (John 6:37). So I know that if I come to you honestly asking for your forgiveness and salvation you will not turn me away. You also say in your Word. "Everyone who calls on the Name of the Lord will be saved." I call on your name now save me Lord Jesus.

Dear Lord, I am sorry for all the wrong I have done in my life and now I turn away from it. I will, with your help begin a new life today and call upon you to help and guide me. I believe in my heart that Jesus Christ is the Son of God and that He died for me closing the gap between me and God. I now accept you as my Lord and Saviour. Amen.